C000157524

Data Access
Complete Self-Assessment Guide

The guidance in this Self-Assessment is based on Data Access best practices and standards in business process architecture, design and quality management. The guidance is also based on the professional judgment of the individual collaborators listed in the Acknowledgments.

Notice of rights

Trademarks

Table of Contents

About The Art of Service

The Art of Service, Business Process Architects since 2000, is dedicated to helping stakeholders achieve excellence.

Defining, designing, creating, and implementing a process to solve a stakeholders challenge or meet an objective is the most valuable role… In EVERY group, company, organization and department.

Unless you're talking a one-time, single-use project, there should be a process. Whether that process is managed and implemented by humans, AI, or a combination of the two, it needs to be designed by someone with a complex enough perspective to ask the right questions.

Someone capable of asking the right questions and step back and say, 'What are we really trying to accomplish here? And is there a different way to look at it?'

With The Art of Service's Standard Requirements Self-Assessments, we empower people who can do just that — whether their title is marketer, entrepreneur, manager, salesperson, consultant, Business Process Manager, executive assistant, IT Manager, CIO etc... —they are the people who rule the future. They are people who watch the process as it happens, and ask the right questions to make the process work better.

Contact us when you need any support with this Self-Assessment and any help with templates, blue-prints and examples of standard documents you might need:

http://theartofservice.com
service@theartofservice.com

Acknowledgments

This checklist was developed under the auspices of The Art of Service, chaired by Gerardus Blokdyk.

Representatives from several client companies participated in the preparation of this Self-Assessment.

In addition, we are thankful for the design and printing services provided.

Included Resources - how to access

Included with your purchase of the book is the Data Access Self-Assessment Spreadsheet Dashboard which contains all questions and Self-Assessment areas and auto-generates insights, graphs, and project RACI planning - all with examples to get you started right away.

How? Simply send an email to
access@theartofservice.com
with this books' title in the subject to get the Data Access Self Assessment Tool right away.

You will receive the following contents with New and Updated specific criteria:

• The latest quick edition of the book in PDF

• The latest complete edition of the book in PDF, which criteria correspond to the criteria in...

• The Self-Assessment Excel Dashboard, and...

• Example pre-filled Self-Assessment Excel Dashboard to get familiar with results generation

• In-depth specific Checklists covering the topic

• Project management checklists and templates to assist with implementation

INCLUDES LIFETIME SELF ASSESSMENT UPDATES

Every self assessment comes with Lifetime Updates and Lifetime Free Updated Books. Lifetime Updates is an industry-first feature which allows you to receive verified self assessment updates, ensuring you always have the most accurate information at your fingertips.

Get it now- you will be glad you did - do it now, before you forget.

Send an email to **access@theartofservice.com** with this books' title in the subject to get the Data Access Self Assessment Tool right away.

Your feedback is invaluable to us

If you recently bought this book, we would love to hear from you! You can do this by writing a review on amazon (or the online store where you purchased this book) about your last purchase! As part of our continual service improvement process, we love to hear real client experiences and feedback.

How does it work?
To post a review on Amazon, just log in to your account and click on the Create Your Own Review button (under Customer Reviews) of the relevant product page. You can find examples of product reviews in Amazon. If you purchased from another online store, simply follow their procedures.

What happens when I submit my review?
Once you have submitted your review, send us an email at review@theartofservice.com with the link to your review so we can properly thank you for your feedback.

Purpose of this Self-Assessment

This Self-Assessment has been developed to improve understanding of the requirements and elements of Data Access, based on best practices and standards in business process architecture, design and quality management.

It is designed to allow for a rapid Self-Assessment to determine how closely existing management practices and procedures correspond to the elements of the Self-Assessment.

The criteria of requirements and elements of Data Access have been rephrased in the format of a Self-Assessment questionnaire, with a seven-criterion scoring system, as explained in this document.

In this format, even with limited background knowledge of

Data Access, a manager can quickly review existing operations to determine how they measure up to the standards. This in turn can serve as the starting point of a 'gap analysis' to identify management tools or system elements that might usefully be implemented in the organization to help improve overall performance.

How to use the Self-Assessment

On the following pages are a series of questions to identify to what extent your Data Access initiative is complete in comparison to the requirements set in standards.

To facilitate answering the questions, there is a space in front of each question to enter a score on a scale of '1' to '5'.

1 Strongly Disagree

2 Disagree

3 Neutral

4 Agree

5 Strongly Agree

Read the question and rate it with the following in front of mind:

**'In my belief,
the answer to this question is clearly defined'.**

There are two ways in which you can choose to interpret this statement;
1. how aware are you that the answer to the question is clearly defined
2. for more in-depth analysis you can choose to gather

evidence and confirm the answer to the question. This obviously will take more time, most Self-Assessment users opt for the first way to interpret the question and dig deeper later on based on the outcome of the overall Self-Assessment.

A score of '1' would mean that the answer is not clear at all, where a '5' would mean the answer is crystal clear and defined. Leave emtpy when the question is not applicable or you don't want to answer it, you can skip it without affecting your score. Write your score in the space provided.

After you have responded to all the appropriate statements in each section, compute your average score for that section, using the formula provided, and round to the nearest tenth. Then transfer to the corresponding spoke in the Data Access Scorecard on the second next page of the Self-Assessment.

Your completed Data Access Scorecard will give you a clear presentation of which Data Access areas need attention.

Data Access
Scorecard Example

Example of how the finalized Scorecard can look like:

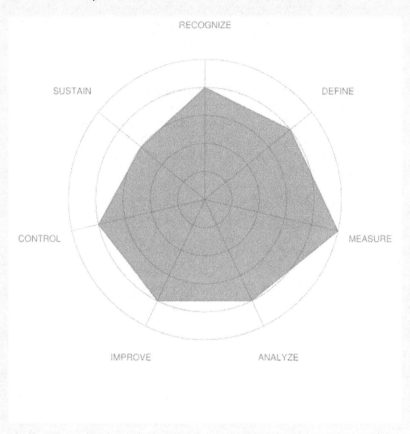

Data Access Scorecard

Your Scores:

BEGINNING OF THE
SELF-ASSESSMENT:

CRITERION #1: RECOGNIZE

INTENT: Be aware of the need for change. Recognize that there is an unfavorable variation, problem or symptom.

In my belief, the answer to this question is clearly defined:

5 Strongly Agree

4 Agree

3 Neutral

2 Disagree

1 Strongly Disagree

1. Is it clear when you think of the day ahead of you what activities and tasks you need to complete?
<--- Score

2. What is the smallest subset of the problem you can usefully solve?
<--- Score

3. How are the data access's objectives aligned to the

group's overall stakeholder strategy?

<--- Score

4. What are your needs in relation to data access skills, labor, equipment, and markets?

<--- Score

5. What problems are you facing and how do you consider data access will circumvent those obstacles?

<--- Score

6. How do you identify subcontractor relationships?

<--- Score

7. As a sponsor, customer or management, how important is it to meet goals, objectives?

<--- Score

8. How do you recognize an data access objection?

<--- Score

9. What are the stakeholder objectives to be achieved with data access?

<--- Score

10. What vendors make products that address the data access needs?

<--- Score

11. Are employees recognized or rewarded for performance that demonstrates the highest levels of integrity?

<--- Score

12. Will data access deliverables need to be tested and, if so, by whom?

<--- Score

13. Why is this needed?
<--- Score

14. What do employees need in the short term?
<--- Score

15. How are you going to measure success?
<--- Score

16. What is the extent or complexity of the data access problem?
<--- Score

17. Are there any specific expectations or concerns about the data access team, data access itself?
<--- Score

18. What are the expected benefits of data access to the stakeholder?
<--- Score

19. What activities does the governance board need to consider?
<--- Score

20. Consider your own data access project, what types of organizational problems do you think might be causing or affecting your problem, based on the work done so far?
<--- Score

21. When a data access manager recognizes a problem, what options are available?
<--- Score

22. What information do users need?
<--- Score

23. How does it fit into your organizational needs and tasks?
<--- Score

24. Whom do you really need or want to serve?
<--- Score

25. Looking at each person individually – does every one have the qualities which are needed to work in this group?
<--- Score

26. Who are your key stakeholders who need to sign off?
<--- Score

27. What prevents you from making the changes you know will make you a more effective data access leader?
<--- Score

28. Which information does the data access business case need to include?
<--- Score

29. Are there data access problems defined?
<--- Score

30. Who needs what information?
<--- Score

31. What is the problem and/or vulnerability?

<--- Score

32. What else needs to be measured?
<--- Score

33. Is the need for organizational change recognized?
<--- Score

34. Are controls defined to recognize and contain problems?
<--- Score

35. Do you know what you need to know about data access?
<--- Score

36. To what extent would your organization benefit from being recognized as a award recipient?
<--- Score

37. Are there any revenue recognition issues?
<--- Score

38. How much are sponsors, customers, partners, stakeholders involved in data access? In other words, what are the risks, if data access does not deliver successfully?
<--- Score

39. How do you recognize an objection?
<--- Score

40. Are employees recognized for desired behaviors?
<--- Score

41. What situation(s) led to this data access Self

Assessment?
<--- Score

42. Who needs budgets?
<--- Score

43. What needs to stay?
<--- Score

44. What tools and technologies are needed for a custom data access project?
<--- Score

45. Are there regulatory / compliance issues?
<--- Score

46. Does your organization need more data access education?
<--- Score

47. What resources or support might you need?
<--- Score

48. What extra resources will you need?
<--- Score

49. Are there recognized data access problems?
<--- Score

50. Have you identified your data access key performance indicators?
<--- Score

51. Who else hopes to benefit from it?
<--- Score

52. What data access capabilities do you need?
<--- Score

53. What is the recognized need?
<--- Score

54. What needs to be done?
<--- Score

55. What are the data access resources needed?
<--- Score

56. Are problem definition and motivation clearly presented?
<--- Score

57. Will it solve real problems?
<--- Score

58. How are training requirements identified?
<--- Score

59. Which issues are too important to ignore?
<--- Score

60. What are the timeframes required to resolve each of the issues/problems?
<--- Score

61. Do you recognize data access achievements?
<--- Score

62. What data access coordination do you need?
<--- Score

63. What creative shifts do you need to take?

<--- Score

64. Who needs to know about data access?
<--- Score

65. To what extent does each concerned units management team recognize data access as an effective investment?
<--- Score

66. What training and capacity building actions are needed to implement proposed reforms?
<--- Score

67. What data access problem should be solved?
<--- Score

68. Think about the people you identified for your data access project and the project responsibilities you would assign to them, what kind of training do you think they would need to perform these responsibilities effectively?
<--- Score

69. Where is training needed?
<--- Score

70. Who needs to know?
<--- Score

71. Is it needed?
<--- Score

72. How many trainings, in total, are needed?
<--- Score

73. What should be considered when identifying available resources, constraints, and deadlines?
<--- Score

74. Who defines the rules in relation to any given issue?
<--- Score

75. How do you assess your data access workforce capability and capacity needs, including skills, competencies, and staffing levels?
<--- Score

76. What are the clients issues and concerns?
<--- Score

77. Is the quality assurance team identified?
<--- Score

78. Where do you need to exercise leadership?
<--- Score

79. Does data access create potential expectations in other areas that need to be recognized and considered?
<--- Score

80. How do you identify the kinds of information that you will need?
<--- Score

81. What are the minority interests and what amount of minority interests can be recognized?
<--- Score

82. How can auditing be a preventative security

measure?
<--- Score

83. Which needs are not included or involved?
<--- Score

84. Do you need to avoid or amend any data access activities?
<--- Score

85. Are your goals realistic? Do you need to redefine your problem? Perhaps the problem has changed or maybe you have reached your goal and need to set a new one?
<--- Score

86. What would happen if data access weren't done?
<--- Score

87. What does data access success mean to the stakeholders?
<--- Score

Add up total points for this section:
_ _ _ _ _ = Total points for this section

Divided by: _ _ _ _ _ _ (number of statements answered) = _ _ _ _ _ _
Average score for this section

Transfer your score to the data access Index at the beginning of the Self-Assessment.

CRITERION #2: DEFINE:

INTENT: Formulate the stakeholder problem. Define the problem, needs and objectives.

In my belief, the answer to this question is clearly defined:

5 Strongly Agree

4 Agree

3 Neutral

2 Disagree

1 Strongly Disagree

1. Who is gathering information?
<--- Score

2. Is the scope of data access defined?
<--- Score

3. How did the data access manager receive input to the development of a data access improvement plan and the estimated completion dates/times of each

activity?
<--- Score

4. Has a project plan, Gantt chart, or similar been developed/completed?
<--- Score

5. Is a fully trained team formed, supported, and committed to work on the data access improvements?
<--- Score

6. What key stakeholder process output measure(s) does data access leverage and how?
<--- Score

7. Are the data access requirements complete?
<--- Score

8. What data access requirements should be gathered?
<--- Score

9. Are approval levels defined for contracts and supplements to contracts?
<--- Score

10. How often are the team meetings?
<--- Score

11. Will team members perform data access work when assigned and in a timely fashion?
<--- Score

12. Has a high-level 'as is' process map been completed, verified and validated?
<--- Score

13. What is out-of-scope initially?
<--- Score

14. Has everyone on the team, including the team leaders, been properly trained?
<--- Score

15. Is the data access scope manageable?
<--- Score

16. Why are you doing data access and what is the scope?
<--- Score

17. What customer feedback methods were used to solicit their input?
<--- Score

18. Is full participation by members in regularly held team meetings guaranteed?
<--- Score

19. Is it clearly defined in and to your organization what you do?
<--- Score

20. Has the direction changed at all during the course of data access? If so, when did it change and why?
<--- Score

21. How have you defined all data access requirements first?
<--- Score

22. What defines best in class?

<--- Score

23. Are accountability and ownership for data access clearly defined?
<--- Score

24. If substitutes have been appointed, have they been briefed on the data access goals and received regular communications as to the progress to date?
<--- Score

25. How do you build the right business case?
<--- Score

26. Scope of sensitive information?
<--- Score

27. Do you have organizational privacy requirements?
<--- Score

28. Is data access required?
<--- Score

29. Is the team adequately staffed with the desired cross-functionality? If not, what additional resources are available to the team?
<--- Score

30. What intelligence can you gather?
<--- Score

31. Is the data access scope complete and appropriately sized?
<--- Score

32. How does the data access manager ensure against

scope creep?
<--- Score

33. What is the definition of success?
<--- Score

34. Will a data access production readiness review be required?
<--- Score

35. What are the rough order estimates on cost savings/opportunities that data access brings?
<--- Score

36. How can the value of data access be defined?
<--- Score

37. What critical content must be communicated – who, what, when, where, and how?
<--- Score

38. What are the dynamics of the communication plan?
<--- Score

39. How do you gather data access requirements?
<--- Score

40. Are there different segments of customers?
<--- Score

41. Do the problem and goal statements meet the SMART criteria (specific, measurable, attainable, relevant, and time-bound)?
<--- Score

42. What information do you gather?
<--- Score

43. Are roles and responsibilities formally defined?
<--- Score

44. How do you think the partners involved in data access would have defined success?
<--- Score

45. Have all basic functions of data access been defined?
<--- Score

46. Has the data access work been fairly and/ or equitably divided and delegated among team members who are qualified and capable to perform the work? Has everyone contributed?
<--- Score

47. Does the team have regular meetings?
<--- Score

48. Is the team sponsored by a champion or stakeholder leader?
<--- Score

49. How do you gather the stories?
<--- Score

50. How do you manage unclear data access requirements?
<--- Score

51. What sources do you use to gather information for a data access study?

<--- Score

52. Has anyone else (internal or external to the group) attempted to solve this problem or a similar one before? If so, what knowledge can be leveraged from these previous efforts?
<--- Score

53. What data access services do you require?
<--- Score

54. Has the improvement team collected the 'voice of the customer' (obtained feedback – qualitative and quantitative)?
<--- Score

55. Do you all define data access in the same way?
<--- Score

56. Is there a completed, verified, and validated high-level 'as is' (not 'should be' or 'could be') stakeholder process map?
<--- Score

57. Has/have the customer(s) been identified?
<--- Score

58. What is the context?
<--- Score

59. What specifically is the problem? Where does it occur? When does it occur? What is its extent?
<--- Score

60. How do you manage scope?
<--- Score

61. How is the team tracking and documenting its work?
<--- Score

62. When is/was the data access start date?
<--- Score

63. Are the data access requirements testable?
<--- Score

64. Is there any additional data access definition of success?
<--- Score

65. How will the data access team and the group measure complete success of data access?
<--- Score

66. Is the work to date meeting requirements?
<--- Score

67. Has your scope been defined?
<--- Score

68. Are team charters developed?
<--- Score

69. Is data access currently on schedule according to the plan?
<--- Score

70. Is there a completed SIPOC representation, describing the Suppliers, Inputs, Process, Outputs, and Customers?
<--- Score

71. Who defines (or who defined) the rules and roles?
<--- Score

72. Is data access linked to key stakeholder goals and objectives?
<--- Score

73. Are all requirements met?
<--- Score

74. What are the compelling stakeholder reasons for embarking on data access?
<--- Score

75. Are customer(s) identified and segmented according to their different needs and requirements?
<--- Score

76. Is the improvement team aware of the different versions of a process: what they think it is vs. what it actually is vs. what it should be vs. what it could be?
<--- Score

77. How was the 'as is' process map developed, reviewed, verified and validated?
<--- Score

78. Is the current 'as is' process being followed? If not, what are the discrepancies?
<--- Score

79. What scope do you want your strategy to cover?
<--- Score

80. What are the data access use cases?

<--- Score

81. Are stakeholder processes mapped?
<--- Score

82. Have the customer needs been translated into specific, measurable requirements? How?
<--- Score

83. What constraints exist that might impact the team?
<--- Score

84. Is there a data access management charter, including stakeholder case, problem and goal statements, scope, milestones, roles and responsibilities, communication plan?
<--- Score

85. How do you gather requirements?
<--- Score

86. Is data collected and displayed to better understand customer(s) critical needs and requirements.
<--- Score

87. How do you catch data access definition inconsistencies?
<--- Score

88. What are the Roles and Responsibilities for each team member and its leadership? Where is this documented?
<--- Score

89. Will team members regularly document their data access work?
<--- Score

90. What is the definition of data access excellence?
<--- Score

91. How do you keep key subject matter experts in the loop?
<--- Score

92. What is a worst-case scenario for losses?
<--- Score

93. Are customers identified and high impact areas defined?
<--- Score

94. Who are the data access improvement team members, including Management Leads and Coaches?
<--- Score

95. Is the team equipped with available and reliable resources?
<--- Score

96. What gets examined?
<--- Score

97. When is the estimated completion date?
<--- Score

98. What baselines are required to be defined and managed?
<--- Score

99. Are different versions of process maps needed to account for the different types of inputs?
<--- Score

100. Are task requirements clearly defined?
<--- Score

101. Are improvement team members fully trained on data access?
<--- Score

102. The political context: who holds power?
<--- Score

103. How do you manage changes in data access requirements?
<--- Score

104. Are resources adequate for the scope?
<--- Score

105. When are meeting minutes sent out? Who is on the distribution list?
<--- Score

106. What would be the goal or target for a data access's improvement team?
<--- Score

107. Are required metrics defined, what are they?
<--- Score

108. What is in the scope and what is not in scope?
<--- Score

109. How and when will the baselines be defined?
<--- Score

110. In what way can you redefine the criteria of choice clients have in your category in your favor?
<--- Score

111. Has a team charter been developed and communicated?
<--- Score

112. What are the boundaries of the scope? What is in bounds and what is not? What is the start point? What is the stop point?
<--- Score

113. How would you define the culture at your organization, how susceptible is it to data access changes?
<--- Score

114. What are the data access tasks and definitions?
<--- Score

115. What knowledge or experience is required?
<--- Score

116. Is there a critical path to deliver data access results?
<--- Score

117. Is there regularly 100% attendance at the team meetings? If not, have appointed substitutes attended to preserve cross-functionality and full representation?
<--- Score

118. Is the team formed and are team leaders (Coaches and Management Leads) assigned?
<--- Score

119. Are there any constraints known that bear on the ability to perform data access work? How is the team addressing them?
<--- Score

120. What was the context?
<--- Score

121. Does the scope remain the same?
<--- Score

122. What are the requirements for audit information?
<--- Score

123. How will variation in the actual durations of each activity be dealt with to ensure that the expected data access results are met?
<--- Score

124. How would you define data access leadership?
<--- Score

Add up total points for this section:
_ _ _ _ _ = Total points for this section

Divided by: _ _ _ _ _ _ (number of statements answered) = _ _ _ _ _ _
Average score for this section

Transfer your score to the data access Index at the beginning of the Self-

Assessment.

CRITERION #3: MEASURE:

INTENT: Gather the correct data.
Measure the current performance and
evolution of the situation.

In my belief, the answer to this
question is clearly defined:

5 Strongly Agree

4 Agree

3 Neutral

2 Disagree

1 Strongly Disagree

1. Are there any easy-to-implement alternatives to data access? Sometimes other solutions are available that do not require the cost implications of a full-blown project?
<--- Score

2. Are you taking your company in the direction of better and revenue or cheaper and cost?
<--- Score

3. What is an unallowable cost?
<--- Score

4. How will measures be used to manage and adapt?
<--- Score

5. What causes mismanagement?
<--- Score

6. How do you quantify and qualify impacts?
<--- Score

7. What is the data access business impact?
<--- Score

8. What is the total cost related to deploying data access, including any consulting or professional services?
<--- Score

9. What causes extra work or rework?
<--- Score

10. What do people want to verify?
<--- Score

11. How do you verify the data access requirements quality?
<--- Score

12. Have the types of risks that may impact data access been identified and analyzed?
<--- Score

13. How do your measurements capture actionable

data access information for use in exceeding your customers expectations and securing your customers engagement?
<--- Score

14. What are the data access key cost drivers?
<--- Score

15. What are the focus and limitations of the data?
<--- Score

16. How will the data access data be analyzed?
<--- Score

17. What relevant entities could be measured?
<--- Score

18. Do staff have the necessary skills to collect, analyze, and report data?
<--- Score

19. Who should receive measurement reports?
<--- Score

20. Are there measurements based on task performance?
<--- Score

21. What is the cost of rework?
<--- Score

22. How is integrated data accessed by analysts?
<--- Score

23. How can you reduce the costs of obtaining inputs?
<--- Score

24. Who is involved in verifying compliance?
<--- Score

25. Does your organization systematically track and analyze outcomes related for accountability and quality improvement?
<--- Score

26. What are the uncertainties surrounding estimates of impact?
<--- Score

27. How are you verifying it?
<--- Score

28. What users will be impacted?
<--- Score

29. What disadvantage does this cause for the user?
<--- Score

30. Are the data access benefits worth its costs?
<--- Score

31. How is progress measured?
<--- Score

32. What impact would the naming conventions have on later data access?
<--- Score

33. Is the scope of data access cost analysis cost-effective?
<--- Score

34. What are the costs of delaying data access action?
<--- Score

35. How do you know that any data access analysis is complete and comprehensive?
<--- Score

36. What causes innovation to fail or succeed in your organization?
<--- Score

37. How are measurements made?
<--- Score

38. Will data access have an impact on current business continuity, disaster recovery processes and/or infrastructure?
<--- Score

39. Do you have an issue in getting priority?
<--- Score

40. How will costs be allocated?
<--- Score

41. What could cause delays in the schedule?
<--- Score

42. How can you measure the performance?
<--- Score

43. Was a business case (cost/benefit) developed?
<--- Score

44. At what cost?
<--- Score

45. What potential environmental factors impact the data access effort?
<--- Score

46. Is the data analysis process consistent with requirements and relevant regulations?
<--- Score

47. What are the operational costs after data access deployment?
<--- Score

48. Who pays the cost?
<--- Score

49. How do you measure variability?
<--- Score

50. What are you verifying?
<--- Score

51. Are there competing data access priorities?
<--- Score

52. How will effects be measured?
<--- Score

53. What are allowable costs?
<--- Score

54. How do you verify the authenticity of the data and information used?
<--- Score

55. What drives O&M cost?

<--- Score

56. How to cause the change?
<--- Score

57. What are the costs and benefits?
<--- Score

58. How much does it cost?
<--- Score

59. Which data access impacts are significant?
<--- Score

60. What is the root cause(s) of the problem?
<--- Score

61. How do you verify and validate the data access data?
<--- Score

62. How do you do risk analysis of rare, cascading, catastrophic events?
<--- Score

63. What are the types and number of measures to use?
<--- Score

64. Is the cost worth the data access effort ?
<--- Score

65. How can a data access test verify your ideas or assumptions?
<--- Score

66. Why do you expend time and effort to implement measurement, for whom?
<--- Score

67. What impact will Software updates have on later data access?
<--- Score

68. What are your key data access organizational performance measures, including key short and longer-term financial measures?
<--- Score

69. How do you focus on what is right -not who is right?
<--- Score

70. Has a cost center been established?
<--- Score

71. What harm might be caused?
<--- Score

72. What is your data access quality cost segregation study?
<--- Score

73. Does the data access task fit the client's priorities?
<--- Score

74. What are the estimated costs of proposed changes?
<--- Score

75. Have you included everything in your data access cost models?

<--- Score

76. How do you verify data access completeness and accuracy?
<--- Score

77. What are your primary costs, revenues, assets?
<--- Score

78. How are costs allocated?
<--- Score

79. Who is responsible for the cost of data sharing?
<--- Score

80. How is the value delivered by data access being measured?
<--- Score

81. How do you verify your resources?
<--- Score

82. How long to keep data and how to manage retention costs?
<--- Score

83. Are you aware of what could cause a problem?
<--- Score

84. How do you measure lifecycle phases?
<--- Score

85. How will success or failure be measured?
<--- Score

86. What would be a real cause for concern?

<--- Score

87. How sensitive must the data access strategy be to cost?
<--- Score

88. What causes investor action?
<--- Score

89. Does data access systematically track and analyze outcomes for accountability and quality improvement?
<--- Score

90. What impact would the naming conventions and the use of homegrown software have on later data access?
<--- Score

91. What are the strategic priorities for this year?
<--- Score

92. Did you tackle the cause or the symptom?
<--- Score

93. What are hidden data access quality costs?
<--- Score

94. Do you aggressively reward and promote the people who have the biggest impact on creating excellent data access services/products?
<--- Score

95. How frequently do you track data access measures?
<--- Score

96. Where is it measured?
<--- Score

97. What are predictive data access analytics?
<--- Score

98. Are you able to realize any cost savings?
<--- Score

99. What does losing customers cost your organization?
<--- Score

100. Do you effectively measure and reward individual and team performance?
<--- Score

101. How can you reduce costs?
<--- Score

102. Have changes been properly/adequately analyzed for effect?
<--- Score

103. How do you control the overall costs of your work processes?
<--- Score

104. Why do you need data analysis?
<--- Score

105. Do you verify that corrective actions were taken?
<--- Score

106. What are your customers expectations and

measures?
<--- Score

107. What measurements are being captured?
<--- Score

108. How do you verify if data access is built right?
<--- Score

109. The approach of traditional data access works for detail complexity but is focused on a systematic approach rather than an understanding of the nature of systems themselves, what approach will permit your organization to deal with the kind of unpredictable emergent behaviors that dynamic complexity can introduce?
<--- Score

110. Where is the cost?
<--- Score

111. Is the solution cost-effective?
<--- Score

112. What does your operating model cost?
<--- Score

113. What is measured? Why?
<--- Score

114. What are the data access investment costs?
<--- Score

115. How will you measure your data access effectiveness?
<--- Score

116. Does management have the right priorities among projects?
<--- Score

117. When a disaster occurs, who gets priority?
<--- Score

118. Are the units of measure consistent?
<--- Score

119. Is all data accessible by business analysts?
<--- Score

120. Are missed data access opportunities costing your organization money?
<--- Score

121. How is performance measured?
<--- Score

122. Are losses documented, analyzed, and remedial processes developed to prevent future losses?
<--- Score

123. What happens if cost savings do not materialize?
<--- Score

124. What are the costs?
<--- Score

125. Is it possible to estimate the impact of unanticipated complexity such as wrong or failed assumptions, feedback, etcetera on proposed reforms?
<--- Score

126. How do you manage public data access costs?
<--- Score

127. Why do the measurements/indicators matter?
<--- Score

128. Are indirect costs charged to the data access program?
<--- Score

129. Do the benefits outweigh the costs?
<--- Score

130. What details are required of the data access cost structure?
<--- Score

131. How can you manage cost down?
<--- Score

132. What are your operating costs?
<--- Score

133. How do you verify and develop ideas and innovations?
<--- Score

134. Are actual costs in line with budgeted costs?
<--- Score

135. How do you measure success?
<--- Score

136. What do you measure and why?
<--- Score

137. Where can you go to verify the info?
<--- Score

138. What measurements are possible, practicable and meaningful?
<--- Score

139. Have the concerns of stakeholders to help identify and define potential barriers been obtained and analyzed?
<--- Score

140. Does data access analysis show the relationships among important data access factors?
<--- Score

141. Is a follow-up focused external data access review required?
<--- Score

Add up total points for this section:
_ _ _ _ _ = Total points for this section

Divided by: _ _ _ _ _ _ (number of statements answered) = _ _ _ _ _ _
Average score for this section

Transfer your score to the data access Index at the beginning of the Self-Assessment.

CRITERION #4: ANALYZE:

INTENT: Analyze causes, assumptions
and hypotheses.

In my belief, the answer to this
question is clearly defined:

5 Strongly Agree

4 Agree

3 Neutral

2 Disagree

1 Strongly Disagree

1. Do staff qualifications match your project?
<--- Score

2. Have you had experiences where canonical modeling was neglected on a data integration project?
<--- Score

3. Have you had experiences where data integration was neglected on a data warehousing

project?
<--- Score

4. How readily is the data accessed and by whom is it used?
<--- Score

5. Will the data be de-identified or anonymized?
<--- Score

6. Is there a clear flight data access and security policy?
<--- Score

7. What qualifications are necessary?
<--- Score

8. Have you had experiences where metadata was neglected on a data integration project?
<--- Score

9. How are you auditing data access: who did what and when?
<--- Score

10. Have you had experiences where particular attention was paid to metadata for data integration?
<--- Score

11. Do several people in different organizational units assist with the data access process?
<--- Score

12. What training and qualifications will you need?
<--- Score

13. How do mission and objectives affect the data access processes of your organization?
<--- Score

14. Does the user have access to all data?
<--- Score

15. Is pre-qualification of suppliers carried out?
<--- Score

16. How difficult is it to qualify what data access ROI is?
<--- Score

17. What systems/processes must you excel at?
<--- Score

18. Data accessibility and location; who has what?
<--- Score

19. What data do you need where and when?
<--- Score

20. How do you provide (automated) support for evolving the system (ontology, mapping, new data sources)?
<--- Score

21. What process should you select for improvement?
<--- Score

22. What are the processes for audit reporting and management?
<--- Score

23. Where will data be archived (preserved)?
<--- Score

24. Should data services be a SaaS or in-house solution?
<--- Score

25. How is the way you as the leader think and process information affecting your organizational culture?
<--- Score

26. Will you be providing self-service access to data or develop a provisioning team?
<--- Score

27. Do your employees have the opportunity to do what they do best everyday?
<--- Score

28. How will you keep track of all the data?
<--- Score

29. What, related to, data access processes does your organization outsource?
<--- Score

30. What strengths and weaknesses do you notice in your data?
<--- Score

31. What kinds of transformations are done to the data being archived?
<--- Score

32. In what country is the data stored when a CSPs solution is in use?

<--- Score

33. Is the data accessible, of high quality and being recorded today?
<--- Score

34. Do you, as a leader, bounce back quickly from setbacks?
<--- Score

35. Is your organization using more than one method to collect data?
<--- Score

36. How do you store data?
<--- Score

37. Have you had experiences where data integration was neglected on a big data project?
<--- Score

38. How quickly should access to the data be provided?
<--- Score

39. How do you promote understanding that opportunity for improvement is not criticism of the status quo, or the people who created the status quo?
<--- Score

40. How will the data be compiled and later stored?
<--- Score

41. What are the principles of ontology/schema design that make it possible to infer expected

linguistic patterns or acceptable grammar for referencing information in the database?
<--- Score

42. Have you had experiences where data integration was neglected on a data archiving project?
<--- Score

43. What do you need to qualify?
<--- Score

44. What are the considerations for real-time update of master data?
<--- Score

45. How can risk management be tied procedurally to process elements?
<--- Score

46. Have you had experiences where particular attention was paid to the xml for data integration?
<--- Score

47. What are your current levels and trends in key measures or indicators of data access product and process performance that are important to and directly serve your customers? How do these results compare with the performance of your competitors and other organizations with similar offerings?
<--- Score

48. What qualifications are needed?
<--- Score

49. What lengths will you go to in trying to gain

access to data you want?
<--- Score

50. How are the data accessed and by whom?
<--- Score

51. Who is involved in the management review process?
<--- Score

52. How long does the data need to be stored?
<--- Score

53. How much is your data worth?
<--- Score

54. What data will you purposefully manage?
<--- Score

55. How much data are necessary?
<--- Score

56. What data should you keep or toss?
<--- Score

57. Who will have access to the data?
<--- Score

58. What type of data should be collected and how frequently will it be collected?
<--- Score

59. Will others need to access the data in the future?
<--- Score

60. When should a process be art not science?
<--- Score

61. What qualifies as competition?
<--- Score

62. Who can access data and what level of detail can they see?
<--- Score

63. How do you protect and share data?
<--- Score

64. What kind of crime could a potential new hire have committed that would not only not disqualify him/her from being hired by your organization, but would actually indicate that he/she might be a particularly good fit?
<--- Score

65. How does the organization define, manage, and improve its data access processes?
<--- Score

66. How does your organization ensure that data management systems and practices contribute to high-quality data?
<--- Score

67. What is your organizations process which leads to recognition of value generation?
<--- Score

68. Are you missing data access opportunities?
<--- Score

69. What kinds of tools or technologies are used to support data integration with hadoop?
<--- Score

70. How can you accelerate access to key data?
<--- Score

71. How do you surface All necessary data to All necessary users, while at the same time maintaining the security of the data?
<--- Score

72. How do you identify specific data access investment opportunities and emerging trends?
<--- Score

73. Do you allow tenants to opt out of having data/ metadata accessed via inspection technologies?
<--- Score

74. To what legal jurisdiction are the data and systems subject?
<--- Score

75. How will the change process be managed?
<--- Score

76. How is the data access Value Stream Mapping managed?
<--- Score

77. When do you use batch data integration versus real-time data integration in a big data project?
<--- Score

78. How do your work systems and key work

processes relate to and capitalize on your core competencies?

<--- Score

79. What are the disruptive data access technologies that enable your organization to radically change your business processes?

<--- Score

80. Do you understand your management processes today?

<--- Score

81. Where do you need real-time data and what specific data should be real-time?

<--- Score

82. Is there any way to speed up the process?

<--- Score

83. How do you measure success for your data strategy?

<--- Score

84. Who will facilitate the team and process?

<--- Score

85. What other organizational variables, such as reward systems or communication systems, affect the performance of this data access process?

<--- Score

86. Can you add value to the current data access decision-making process (largely qualitative) by incorporating uncertainty modeling (more quantitative)?

<--- Score

87. Think about the functions involved in your data access project, what processes flow from these functions?
<--- Score

88. What are the best opportunities for value improvement?
<--- Score

89. Identify an operational issue in your organization, for example, could a particular task be done more quickly or more efficiently by data access?
<--- Score

90. Who is involved with workflow mapping?
<--- Score

91. What level of data quality is practical?
<--- Score

92. Are all team members qualified for all tasks?
<--- Score

93. How do you structure data?
<--- Score

94. What are your Data Access Speeds and what testing supports your claims?
<--- Score

95. How long should the data be kept, and who should keep them?
<--- Score

96. How long is this data maintained?
<--- Score

97. How will you address new data sources in the future?
<--- Score

98. What data will you keep?
<--- Score

99. How do you access, share and manage data?
<--- Score

100. What are your current levels and trends in key data access measures or indicators of product and process performance that are important to and directly serve your customers?
<--- Score

101. What is the Value Stream Mapping?
<--- Score

102. Have you seen any data integration projects where xml issues led to significant problems?
<--- Score

103. Is the suppliers process defined and controlled?
<--- Score

104. What are your best practices for minimizing data access project risk, while demonstrating incremental value and quick wins throughout the data access project lifecycle?
<--- Score

105. Are project restrictions on system and data

access creating barriers to task completion?
<--- Score

106. What qualifications do data access leaders need?
<--- Score

107. What patterns do you see in the data?
<--- Score

108. How is data shared between the various data silos?
<--- Score

109. Have you seen any big data projects where data integration issues led to significant problems?
<--- Score

110. How long should you keep the data?
<--- Score

111. Data access and ownership: Who will have access to the data?
<--- Score

112. Is this use of the data appropriate?
<--- Score

113. How do you integrate data silos?
<--- Score

114. How will you measure data quality?
<--- Score

115. Are data sharing and privacy protection mutually exclusive?

<--- Score

116. Who ensures that the data architecture will be updated as evolving data types and needs arise?
<--- Score

117. How will you collect and integrate data over a period of time?
<--- Score

118. Do the applications encrypt data before sending it over the Internet or an open network?
<--- Score

119. Who gets to determine your policies for the maintenance and archival of historic data?
<--- Score

120. Does your data strategy answer the question whether to store data on premise or in the cloud?
<--- Score

121. What is the oversight process?
<--- Score

122. What internal processes need improvement?
<--- Score

123. How do you measure the operational performance of your key work systems and processes, including productivity, cycle time, and other appropriate measures of process effectiveness, efficiency, and innovation?
<--- Score

124. Are the tools for data archiving different for

structured and unstructured data?
<--- Score

125. Is there a strict change management process?
<--- Score

126. How does your organization protect employee identifiable data?
<--- Score

127. Do your leaders quickly bounce back from setbacks?
<--- Score

128. What are your key performance measures or indicators and in-process measures for the control and improvement of your data access processes?
<--- Score

129. Have you seen any projects using hadoop where data integration issues led to significant problems?
<--- Score

130. How are the technologies for metadata, especially around data integration changing?
<--- Score

131. Can the archived data be retrieved?
<--- Score

132. What type of person data or other confidential data is stored on your system?
<--- Score

Add up total points for this section:

_____ = Total points for this section

Divided by: _____ (number of
statements answered) = _____
Average score for this section

Transfer your score to the data access
Index at the beginning of the Self-
Assessment.

CRITERION #5: IMPROVE:

INTENT: Develop a practical solution. Innovate, establish and test the solution and to measure the results.

In my belief, the answer to this question is clearly defined:

5 Strongly Agree

4 Agree

3 Neutral

2 Disagree

1 Strongly Disagree

1. To what extent does management recognize data access as a tool to increase the results?
<--- Score

2. Is pilot data collected and analyzed?
<--- Score

3. Are the best solutions selected?
<--- Score

4. How will the group know that the solution worked?
<--- Score

5. How will you recognize and celebrate results?
<--- Score

6. Where do you need data access improvement?
<--- Score

7. What are the concrete data access results?
<--- Score

8. What alternative responses are available to manage risk?
<--- Score

9. How do you link measurement and risk?
<--- Score

10. What needs improvement? Why?
<--- Score

11. How is continuous improvement applied to risk management?
<--- Score

12. What practices helps your organization to develop its capacity to recognize patterns?
<--- Score

13. Is any data access documentation required?
<--- Score

14. Who are the people involved in developing and implementing data access?

<--- Score

15. Is there a small-scale pilot for proposed improvement(s)? What conclusions were drawn from the outcomes of a pilot?
<--- Score

16. What criteria will you use to assess your data access risks?
<--- Score

17. Is there any other data access solution?
<--- Score

18. What improvements have been achieved?
<--- Score

19. What are the implications of the one critical data access decision 10 minutes, 10 months, and 10 years from now?
<--- Score

20. Is supporting data access documentation required?
<--- Score

21. Is a solution implementation plan established, including schedule/work breakdown structure, resources, risk management plan, cost/budget, and control plan?
<--- Score

22. What attendant changes will need to be made to ensure that the solution is successful?
<--- Score

23. How will you measure the results?
<--- Score

24. What document management components are included in the architecture?
<--- Score

25. How risky is your organization?
<--- Score

26. What is the magnitude of the improvements?
<--- Score

27. Risk Identification: What are the possible risk events your organization faces in relation to data access?
<--- Score

28. Is risk periodically assessed?
<--- Score

29. What assumptions are made about the solution and approach?
<--- Score

30. Are improved process ('should be') maps modified based on pilot data and analysis?
<--- Score

31. What tools were used to evaluate the potential solutions?
<--- Score

32. What is data access's impact on utilizing the best solution(s)?
<--- Score

33. Was a pilot designed for the proposed solution(s)?
<--- Score

34. How can the phases of data access development be identified?
<--- Score

35. Are risk management tasks balanced centrally and locally?
<--- Score

36. What risks do you need to manage?
<--- Score

37. Who controls the risk?
<--- Score

38. Are the most efficient solutions problem-specific?
<--- Score

39. What is data access risk?
<--- Score

40. Do you have the optimal project management team structure?
<--- Score

41. Who should make the data access decisions?
<--- Score

42. Are possible solutions generated and tested?
<--- Score

43. What resources are required for the improvement efforts?

<--- Score

44. What are the affordable data access risks?
<--- Score

45. Can the solution be designed and implemented within an acceptable time period?
<--- Score

46. Is the scope clearly documented?
<--- Score

47. What is the data access's sustainability risk?
<--- Score

48. data access risk decisions: whose call Is It?
<--- Score

49. Are there any constraints (technical, political, cultural, or otherwise) that would inhibit certain solutions?
<--- Score

50. What strategies for data access improvement are successful?
<--- Score

51. Was a data access charter developed?
<--- Score

52. Is there a cost/benefit analysis of optimal solution(s)?
<--- Score

53. How will the team or the process owner(s) monitor the implementation plan to see that it is working as

intended?
<--- Score

54. What does the 'should be' process map/design look like?
<--- Score

55. What error proofing will be done to address some of the discrepancies observed in the 'as is' process?
<--- Score

56. Are new and improved process ('should be') maps developed?
<--- Score

57. Do you cover the five essential competencies: Communication, Collaboration,Innovation, Adaptability, and Leadership that improve an organizations ability to leverage the new data access in a volatile global economy?
<--- Score

58. Which of the recognised risks out of all risks can be most likely transferred?
<--- Score

59. Are decisions made in a timely manner?
<--- Score

60. How is knowledge sharing about risk management improved?
<--- Score

61. Who will be responsible for documenting the data access requirements in detail?
<--- Score

62. How do you keep improving data access?
<--- Score

63. What is the team's contingency plan for potential problems occurring in implementation?
<--- Score

64. What are the expected data access results?
<--- Score

65. Risk factors: what are the characteristics of data access that make it risky?
<--- Score

66. Is the implementation plan designed?
<--- Score

67. Who are the data access decision-makers?
<--- Score

68. Have you achieved data access improvements?
<--- Score

69. How do you improve data access service perception, and satisfaction?
<--- Score

70. What can you do to improve?
<--- Score

71. Do you combine technical expertise with business knowledge and data access Key topics include lifecycles, development approaches, requirements and how to make a business case?
<--- Score

72. Who manages data access risk?
<--- Score

73. Who manages supplier risk management in your organization?
<--- Score

74. How do you go about comparing data access approaches/solutions?
<--- Score

75. Are the key business and technology risks being managed?
<--- Score

76. What lessons, if any, from a pilot were incorporated into the design of the full-scale solution?
<--- Score

77. How do you measure improved data access service perception, and satisfaction?
<--- Score

78. How do you define the solutions' scope?
<--- Score

79. Where do the data access decisions reside?
<--- Score

80. How do you improve your likelihood of success ?
<--- Score

81. What tools were most useful during the improve phase?
<--- Score

82. Is the data access solution sustainable?
<--- Score

83. What is the implementation plan?
<--- Score

84. Who are the data access decision makers?
<--- Score

85. Are procedures documented for managing data access risks?
<--- Score

86. What tools were used to tap into the creativity and encourage 'outside the box' thinking?
<--- Score

87. How did the team generate the list of possible solutions?
<--- Score

88. What data access improvements can be made?
<--- Score

89. Is a contingency plan established?
<--- Score

90. Would you develop a data access Communication Strategy?
<--- Score

91. How will you know when its improved?
<--- Score

92. What went well, what should change, what can

improve?
<--- Score

93. Who controls key decisions that will be made?
<--- Score

94. What is the risk?
<--- Score

95. What actually has to improve and by how much?
<--- Score

96. What were the underlying assumptions on the cost-benefit analysis?
<--- Score

97. How will you know that a change is an improvement?
<--- Score

98. Who makes the data access decisions in your organization?
<--- Score

99. Do the viable solutions scale to future needs?
<--- Score

100. Do those selected for the data access team have a good general understanding of what data access is all about?
<--- Score

101. Is data access documentation maintained?
<--- Score

102. Who do you report data access results to?

<--- Score

103. How can you improve performance?
<--- Score

104. Are the risks fully understood, reasonable and manageable?
<--- Score

105. Describe the design of the pilot and what tests were conducted, if any?
<--- Score

106. Will the controls trigger any other risks?
<--- Score

107. How can you improve data access?
<--- Score

108. How are policy decisions made and where?
<--- Score

109. How do you deal with data access risk?
<--- Score

110. Can you integrate quality management and risk management?
<--- Score

111. How do you measure progress and evaluate training effectiveness?
<--- Score

112. How do you mitigate data access risk?
<--- Score

113. How do you manage data access risk?
<--- Score

114. How does the solution remove the key sources of issues discovered in the analyze phase?
<--- Score

115. Is the data access risk managed?
<--- Score

116. Have you identified breakpoints and/or risk tolerances that will trigger broad consideration of a potential need for intervention or modification of strategy?
<--- Score

117. For decision problems, how do you develop a decision statement?
<--- Score

118. Is the data access documentation thorough?
<--- Score

119. What are the data access security risks?
<--- Score

120. What current systems have to be understood and/or changed?
<--- Score

121. How can you better manage risk?
<--- Score

122. Were any criteria developed to assist the team in testing and evaluating potential solutions?
<--- Score

123. Which data access solution is appropriate?
<--- Score

124. What to do with the results or outcomes of measurements?
<--- Score

125. How does the team improve its work?
<--- Score

126. Explorations of the frontiers of data access will help you build influence, improve data access, optimize decision making, and sustain change, what is your approach?
<--- Score

127. Does the goal represent a desired result that can be measured?
<--- Score

128. What communications are necessary to support the implementation of the solution?
<--- Score

129. Is the optimal solution selected based on testing and analysis?
<--- Score

130. How significant is the improvement in the eyes of the end user?
<--- Score

131. Is the measure of success for data access understandable to a variety of people?
<--- Score

Add up total points for this section:
_____ = Total points for this section

Divided by: _____ (number of
statements answered) = _____
Average score for this section

Transfer your score to the data access
Index at the beginning of the Self-
Assessment.

CRITERION #6: CONTROL:

INTENT: Implement the practical solution. Maintain the performance and correct possible complications.

In my belief, the answer to this question is clearly defined:

5 Strongly Agree

4 Agree

3 Neutral

2 Disagree

1 Strongly Disagree

1. Who controls critical resources?
<--- Score

2. How does your organizations policy take into account international data access and privacy standards?
<--- Score

3. Have new or revised work instructions resulted?

<--- Score

4. How will report readings be checked to effectively monitor performance?
<--- Score

5. Can support from partners be adjusted?
<--- Score

6. Does the response plan contain a definite closed loop continual improvement scheme (e.g., plan-do-check-act)?
<--- Score

7. Will any special training be provided for results interpretation?
<--- Score

8. How do you encourage people to take control and responsibility?
<--- Score

9. What are customers monitoring?
<--- Score

10. Are new process steps, standards, and documentation ingrained into normal operations?
<--- Score

11. Is there a control plan in place for sustaining improvements (short and long-term)?
<--- Score

12. Is a plan for Data Management required if a project is not expected to generate data or samples?

<--- Score

13. Are the planned controls in place?
<--- Score

14. How likely is the current data access plan to come in on schedule or on budget?
<--- Score

15. What is the control/monitoring plan?
<--- Score

16. How might the group capture best practices and lessons learned so as to leverage improvements?
<--- Score

17. Are controls in place and consistently applied?
<--- Score

18. Are resources allocated to support the planning, implementation, evaluation and quality assurance of data language services?
<--- Score

19. Can you adapt and adjust to changing data access situations?
<--- Score

20. How will the process owner and team be able to hold the gains?
<--- Score

21. What other systems, operations, processes, and infrastructures (hiring practices, staffing, training, incentives/rewards, metrics/dashboards/scorecards, etc.) need updates, additions, changes, or deletions

in order to facilitate knowledge transfer and improvements?

<--- Score

22. Who will be in control?

<--- Score

23. What other areas of the group might benefit from the data access team's improvements, knowledge, and learning?

<--- Score

24. How do you select, collect, align, and integrate data access data and information for tracking daily operations and overall organizational performance, including progress relative to strategic objectives and action plans?

<--- Score

25. Are pertinent alerts monitored, analyzed and distributed to appropriate personnel?

<--- Score

26. Will the team be available to assist members in planning investigations?

<--- Score

27. Are documented procedures clear and easy to follow for the operators?

<--- Score

28. What should the next improvement project be that is related to data access?

<--- Score

29. What data access standards are applicable?

<--- Score

30. Are operating procedures consistent?
<--- Score

31. How do you plan for the cost of succession?
<--- Score

32. Who is the data access process owner?
<--- Score

33. Are suggested corrective/restorative actions indicated on the response plan for known causes to problems that might surface?
<--- Score

34. Will existing staff require re-training, for example, to learn new business processes?
<--- Score

35. What are your results for key measures or indicators of the accomplishment of your data access strategy and action plans, including building and strengthening core competencies?
<--- Score

36. How will new or emerging customer needs/requirements be checked/communicated to orient the process toward meeting the new specifications and continually reducing variation?
<--- Score

37. Is there a documented and implemented monitoring plan?
<--- Score

38. How do you plan on providing proper recognition and disclosure of supporting companies?
<--- Score

39. What can you control?
<--- Score

40. Is new knowledge gained imbedded in the response plan?
<--- Score

41. Does a troubleshooting guide exist or is it needed?
<--- Score

42. Do you monitor the data access decisions made and fine tune them as they evolve?
<--- Score

43. Are there documented procedures?
<--- Score

44. How do you monitor usage and cost?
<--- Score

45. What are the data access standards and procedures?
<--- Score

46. Are the planned controls working?
<--- Score

47. Does data access appropriately measure and monitor risk?
<--- Score

48. Do employees within your organization prefer

to create documents, spreadsheets, or PDF files?
<--- Score

49. What is your theory of human motivation, and how does your compensation plan fit with that view?
<--- Score

50. Who has control over resources?
<--- Score

51. Has the improved process and its steps been standardized?
<--- Score

52. What are the critical parameters to watch?
<--- Score

53. What should you measure to verify efficiency gains?
<--- Score

54. What is the best design framework for data access organization now that, in a post industrial-age if the top-down, command and control model is no longer relevant?
<--- Score

55. Do you monitor the effectiveness of your data access activities?
<--- Score

56. In the case of a data access project, the criteria for the audit derive from implementation objectives, an audit of a data access project involves assessing whether the recommendations outlined for implementation have been met, can you track that

any data access project is implemented as planned, and is it working?
<--- Score

57. What are the data access standards and procedures in use?
<--- Score

58. Is there documentation that will support the successful operation of the improvement?
<--- Score

59. What is your plan to assess your security risks?
<--- Score

60. What key inputs and outputs are being measured on an ongoing basis?
<--- Score

61. What are the implications of tracking/ monitoring data access?
<--- Score

62. Who sets the data access standards?
<--- Score

63. Is there a recommended audit plan for routine surveillance inspections of data access's gains?
<--- Score

64. How do controls support value?
<--- Score

65. What are the known security controls?
<--- Score

66. Has the data access value of standards been quantified?
<--- Score

67. Is knowledge gained on process shared and institutionalized?
<--- Score

68. Act/Adjust: What Do you Need to Do Differently?
<--- Score

69. Is there a standardized process?
<--- Score

70. What is the standard for acceptable data access performance?
<--- Score

71. Is a response plan in place for when the input, process, or output measures indicate an 'out-of-control' condition?
<--- Score

72. Does activity monitoring include data access i.e. who is accessing the data and what they are doing with the data?
<--- Score

73. What adjustments to the strategies are needed?
<--- Score

74. What are you attempting to measure/monitor?
<--- Score

75. Is there an action plan in case of emergencies?
<--- Score

76. What is the recommended frequency of auditing?
<--- Score

77. How is change control managed?
<--- Score

78. Implementation Planning: is a pilot needed to test the changes before a full roll out occurs?
<--- Score

79. Is a response plan established and deployed?
<--- Score

80. Activity monitoring; does it include data access i.e. who is accessing the data and what they are doing with the data?
<--- Score

81. How will data access decisions be made and monitored?
<--- Score

82. What are the key elements of your data access performance improvement system, including your evaluation, organizational learning, and innovation processes?
<--- Score

83. How will the process owner verify improvement in present and future sigma levels, process capabilities?
<--- Score

84. Is there a transfer of ownership and knowledge to process owner and process team tasked with the responsibilities.

<--- Score

85. Does the data access performance meet the customer's requirements?
<--- Score

86. How will input, process, and output variables be checked to detect for sub-optimal conditions?
<--- Score

87. What quality tools were useful in the control phase?
<--- Score

88. How widespread is its use?
<--- Score

89. How will the day-to-day responsibilities for monitoring and continual improvement be transferred from the improvement team to the process owner?
<--- Score

90. What constitutes data covered by your Data Management Plan?
<--- Score

91. Does job training on the documented procedures need to be part of the process team's education and training?
<--- Score

92. What do you stand for--and what are you against?
<--- Score

93. Is there a data access Communication plan .

covering who needs to get what information when?
<--- Score

94. Are you measuring, monitoring and predicting data access activities to optimize operations and profitability, and enhancing outcomes?
<--- Score

95. How can you best use all of your knowledge repositories to enhance learning and sharing?
<--- Score

96. What are the data access requirements for standard file, message, and data management?
<--- Score

97. Is reporting being used or needed?
<--- Score

98. How is data access project cost planned, managed, monitored?
<--- Score

Add up total points for this section:
_ _ _ _ _ = Total points for this section

Divided by: _ _ _ _ _ _ (number of statements answered) = _ _ _ _ _ _
Average score for this section

Transfer your score to the data access Index at the beginning of the Self-Assessment.

CRITERION #7: SUSTAIN:

INTENT: Retain the benefits.

In my belief, the answer to this question is clearly defined:

5 Strongly Agree

4 Agree

3 Neutral

2 Disagree

1 Strongly Disagree

1. What are the business goals data access is aiming to achieve?
<--- Score

2. Why is it important to have senior management support for a data access project?
<--- Score

3. How do you accomplish your long range data access goals?
<--- Score

4. Who uses your product in ways you never expected?
<--- Score

5. How do you keep records, of what?
<--- Score

6. Who have you, as a company, historically been when you've been at your best?
<--- Score

7. Will there be any necessary staff changes (redundancies or new hires)?
<--- Score

8. What will be the consequences to the stakeholder (financial, reputation etc) if data access does not go ahead or fails to deliver the objectives?
<--- Score

9. Do you think data access accomplishes the goals you expect it to accomplish?
<--- Score

10. Were lessons learned captured and communicated?
<--- Score

11. Is there a work around that you can use?
<--- Score

12. What is it like to work for you?
<--- Score

13. Whose voice (department, ethnic group, women,

older workers, etc) might you have missed hearing from in your company, and how might you amplify this voice to create positive momentum for your business?
<--- Score

14. Are there any activities that you can take off your to do list?
<--- Score

15. What is the range of capabilities?
<--- Score

16. How does data access integrate with other stakeholder initiatives?
<--- Score

17. How do you go about securing data access?
<--- Score

18. How do you listen to customers to obtain actionable information?
<--- Score

19. Who are your customers?
<--- Score

20. What do we do when new problems arise?
<--- Score

21. Are you making progress, and are you making progress as data access leaders?
<--- Score

22. Where can you break convention?
<--- Score

23. When information truly is ubiquitous, when reach and connectivity are completely global, when computing resources are infinite, and when a whole new set of impossibilities are not only possible, but happening, what will that do to your business?
<--- Score

24. What are current data access paradigms?
<--- Score

25. Which data access goals are the most important?
<--- Score

26. What is your BATNA (best alternative to a negotiated agreement)?
<--- Score

27. Are you relevant? Will you be relevant five years from now? Ten?
<--- Score

28. In retrospect, of the projects that you pulled the plug on, what percent do you wish had been allowed to keep going, and what percent do you wish had ended earlier?
<--- Score

29. Did your employees make progress today?
<--- Score

30. How long will it take to change?
<--- Score

31. How do you ensure that implementations of data access products are done in a way that ensures safety?

<--- Score

32. Do you have enough freaky customers in your portfolio pushing you to the limit day in and day out?
<--- Score

33. What should you stop doing?
<--- Score

34. If you got fired and a new hire took your place, what would she do different?
<--- Score

35. Which individuals, teams or departments will be involved in data access?
<--- Score

36. How do you proactively clarify deliverables and data access quality expectations?
<--- Score

37. Can you maintain your growth without detracting from the factors that have contributed to your success?
<--- Score

38. Which functions and people interact with the supplier and or customer?
<--- Score

39. What counts that you are not counting?
<--- Score

40. What is the purpose of data access in relation to the mission?
<--- Score

41. Are new benefits received and understood?
<--- Score

42. Can you break it down?
<--- Score

43. If you had to leave your organization for a year and the only communication you could have with employees/colleagues was a single paragraph, what would you write?
<--- Score

44. Who do you think the world wants your organization to be?
<--- Score

45. When should you bother with diagrams?
<--- Score

46. What happens when a new employee joins the organization?
<--- Score

47. What are your personal philosophies regarding data access and how do they influence your work?
<--- Score

48. Instead of going to current contacts for new ideas, what if you reconnected with dormant contacts-- the people you used to know? If you were going reactivate a dormant tie, who would it be?
<--- Score

49. How much does data access help?
<--- Score

50. If you had to rebuild your organization without any traditional competitive advantages (i.e., no killer technology, promising research, innovative product/ service delivery model, etcetera), how would your people have to approach their work and collaborate together in order to create the necessary conditions for success?
<--- Score

51. What are the success criteria that will indicate that data access objectives have been met and the benefits delivered?
<--- Score

52. Political -is anyone trying to undermine this project?
<--- Score

53. Can the schedule be done in the given time?
<--- Score

54. What does your signature ensure?
<--- Score

55. How do you foster innovation?
<--- Score

56. If you were responsible for initiating and implementing major changes in your organization, what steps might you take to ensure acceptance of those changes?
<--- Score

57. Have new benefits been realized?
<--- Score

58. How do you govern and fulfill your societal responsibilities?
<--- Score

59. What would you recommend your friend do if he/she were facing this dilemma?
<--- Score

60. Who is on the team?
<--- Score

61. How is implementation research currently incorporated into each of your goals?
<--- Score

62. What is the funding source for this project?
<--- Score

63. Is maximizing data access protection the same as minimizing data access loss?
<--- Score

64. What projects are going on in the organization today, and what resources are those projects using from the resource pools?
<--- Score

65. Are the criteria for selecting recommendations stated?
<--- Score

66. What are the usability implications of data access actions?
<--- Score

67. Who are the key stakeholders?
<--- Score

68. Has implementation been effective in reaching specified objectives so far?
<--- Score

69. How do you maintain data access's Integrity?
<--- Score

70. Who do we want your customers to become?
<--- Score

71. What are the potential basics of data access fraud?
<--- Score

72. What happens if you do not have enough funding?
<--- Score

73. Are you using a design thinking approach and integrating Innovation, data access Experience, and Brand Value?
<--- Score

74. What knowledge, skills and characteristics mark a good data access project manager?
<--- Score

75. In the past year, what have you done (or could you have done) to increase the accurate perception of your company/brand as ethical and honest?
<--- Score

76. What management system can you use to leverage the data access experience, ideas, and

concerns of the people closest to the work to be done?
<--- Score

77. Who will determine interim and final deadlines?
<--- Score

78. Are your responses positive or negative?
<--- Score

79. Do you think you know, or do you know you know ?
<--- Score

80. What relationships among data access trends do you perceive?
<--- Score

81. What role does communication play in the success or failure of a data access project?
<--- Score

82. What is the estimated value of the project?
<--- Score

83. Are the assumptions believable and achievable?
<--- Score

84. How do you manage data access Knowledge Management (KM)?
<--- Score

85. Do you know what you are doing? And who do you call if you don't?
<--- Score

86. What do your reports reflect?
<--- Score

87. What one word do you want to own in the minds of your customers, employees, and partners?
<--- Score

88. If no one would ever find out about your accomplishments, how would you lead differently?
<--- Score

89. How do you make it meaningful in connecting data access with what users do day-to-day?
<--- Score

90. How will you motivate the stakeholders with the least vested interest?
<--- Score

91. Does your organization have a formal IT Security team and incident response program?
<--- Score

92. How are you doing compared to your industry?
<--- Score

93. Do data access rules make a reasonable demand on a users capabilities?
<--- Score

94. What is something you believe that nearly no one agrees with you on?
<--- Score

95. Why should you adopt a data access framework?
<--- Score

96. Who else should you help?
<--- Score

97. Are you maintaining a past–present–future perspective throughout the data access discussion?
<--- Score

98. What is your data access strategy?
<--- Score

99. If your customer were your grandmother, would you tell her to buy what you're selling?
<--- Score

100. What is the overall talent health of your organization as a whole at senior levels, and for each organization reporting to a member of the Senior Leadership Team?
<--- Score

101. How do you engage the workforce, in addition to satisfying them?
<--- Score

102. To whom do you add value?
<--- Score

103. Ask yourself: how would you do this work if you only had one staff member to do it?
<--- Score

104. Who is responsible for errors?
<--- Score

105. Can you do all this work?

<--- Score

106. Why not do data access?
<--- Score

107. Have benefits been optimized with all key stakeholders?
<--- Score

108. Operational - will it work?
<--- Score

109. Who are four people whose careers you have enhanced?
<--- Score

110. How do you cross-sell and up-sell your data access success?
<--- Score

111. What could happen if you do not do it?
<--- Score

112. Do you have an implicit bias for capital investments over people investments?
<--- Score

113. What is an unauthorized commitment?
<--- Score

114. Are all key stakeholders present at all Structured Walkthroughs?
<--- Score

115. What potential megatrends could make your business model obsolete?

<--- Score

116. What trouble can you get into?
<--- Score

117. Are assumptions made in data access stated explicitly?
<--- Score

118. What threat is data access addressing?
<--- Score

119. What business benefits will data access goals deliver if achieved?
<--- Score

120. In a project to restructure data access outcomes, which stakeholders would you involve?
<--- Score

121. What is the overall business strategy?
<--- Score

122. Do you see more potential in people than they do in themselves?
<--- Score

123. Would you rather sell to knowledgeable and informed customers or to uninformed customers?
<--- Score

124. Are there state laws that may restrict the exchange of certain kinds of health information?
<--- Score

125. Who is the main stakeholder, with ultimate

responsibility for driving data access forward?
<--- Score

126. Is there any reason to believe the opposite of my current belief?
<--- Score

127. How do you know if you are successful?
<--- Score

128. How can you negotiate data access successfully with a stubborn boss, an irate client, or a deceitful coworker?
<--- Score

129. Is a data access team work effort in place?
<--- Score

130. Is your basic point _____ or _____?
<--- Score

131. What is the source of the strategies for data access strengthening and reform?
<--- Score

132. How do you stay inspired?
<--- Score

133. What are the challenges?
<--- Score

134. Do you feel that more should be done in the data access area?
<--- Score

135. How do you determine the key elements that

affect data access workforce satisfaction, how are these elements determined for different workforce groups and segments?
<--- Score

136. How important is data access to the user organizations mission?
<--- Score

137. If you weren't already in this business, would you enter it today? And if not, what are you going to do about it?
<--- Score

138. Who do you want your customers to become?
<--- Score

139. Whom among your colleagues do you trust, and for what?
<--- Score

140. Staff customer service - is your staff courteous and knowledgeable?
<--- Score

141. What are strategies for increasing support and reducing opposition?
<--- Score

142. Will it be accepted by users?
<--- Score

143. How much contingency will be available in the budget?
<--- Score

144. How do you track customer value, profitability or financial return, organizational success, and sustainability?
<--- Score

145. What is a feasible sequencing of reform initiatives over time?
<--- Score

146. What did you miss in the interview for the worst hire you ever made?
<--- Score

147. What is your competitive advantage?
<--- Score

148. What are specific data access rules to follow?
<--- Score

149. What are you trying to prove to yourself, and how might it be hijacking your life and business success?
<--- Score

150. At what moment would you think; Will I get fired?
<--- Score

151. How do you transition from the baseline to the target?
<--- Score

152. How will you know that the data access project has been successful?
<--- Score

153. Who is responsible for data access?
<--- Score

154. Do you have the right capabilities and capacities?
<--- Score

155. Who will provide the final approval of data access deliverables?
<--- Score

156. What trophy do you want on your mantle?
<--- Score

157. Who is responsible for ensuring appropriate resources (time, people and money) are allocated to data access?
<--- Score

158. Is it economical; do you have the time and money?
<--- Score

159. What stupid rule would you most like to kill?
<--- Score

160. What have you done to protect your business from competitive encroachment?
<--- Score

161. What data access modifications can you make work for you?
<--- Score

162. How do you set data access stretch targets and how do you get people to not only participate in setting these stretch targets but also that they strive to achieve these?
<--- Score

163. What was the last experiment you ran?
<--- Score

164. How do customers see your organization?
<--- Score

165. Why will customers want to buy your organizations products/services?
<--- Score

166. How do you provide a safe environment -physically and emotionally?
<--- Score

167. What would have to be true for the option on the table to be the best possible choice?
<--- Score

168. Why is data access important for you now?
<--- Score

169. Which models, tools and techniques are necessary?
<--- Score

170. How do you foster the skills, knowledge, talents, attributes, and characteristics you want to have?
<--- Score

171. What is your question? Why?
<--- Score

172. If you do not follow, then how to lead?
<--- Score

173. What is the craziest thing you can do?
<--- Score

174. What is effective data access?
<--- Score

175. Is the impact that data access has shown?
<--- Score

Add up total points for this section:
_____ = Total points for this section

Divided by: _____ (number of
statements answered) = _____
Average score for this section

Transfer your score to the data access
Index at the beginning of the Self-
Assessment.

Data Access and Managing Projects, Criteria for Project Managers:

1.0 Initiating Process Group: Data Access

1. When will the Data Access project be done?

2. If the risk event occurs, what will you do?

3. Have the stakeholders identified all individual requirements pertaining to business process?

4. What are the inputs required to produce the deliverables?

5. What will you do to minimize the impact should a risk event occur?

6. At which cmmi level are software processes documented, standardized, and integrated into a standard to-be practiced process for your organization?

7. Do you understand the quality and control criteria that must be achieved for successful Data Access project completion?

8. What input will you be required to provide the Data Access project team?

9. Do you know the roles & responsibilities required for this Data Access project?

10. What do they need to know about the Data Access project?

11. How will it affect me?

12. What communication items need improvement?

13. How should needs be met?

14. Did the Data Access project team have the right skills?

15. What were the challenges that you encountered during the execution of a previous Data Access project that you would not want to repeat?

16. The Data Access project you are managing has nine stakeholders. How many channel of communications are there between corresponding stakeholders?

17. What are the required resources?

18. Who is involved in each phase?

19. At which stage, in a typical Data Access project do stake holders have maximum influence?

20. How will you do it?

1.1 Project Charter: Data Access

21. What are some examples of a business case?

22. Why is it important?

23. Why have you chosen the aim you have set forth?

24. Where and how does the team fit within your organization structure?

25. What are the deliverables?

26. When?

27. Are you building in-house ?

28. Who is the sponsor?

29. Avoid costs, improve service, and/ or comply with a mandate?

30. Why use a Data Access project charter?

31. How are Data Access projects different from operations?

32. Why do you need to manage scope?

33. How will you learn more about the process or system you are trying to improve?

34. Who ise input and support will this Data Access project require?

35. What are the assumptions?

36. Must Have?

37. Is it an improvement over existing products?

38. When will this occur?

39. Assumptions: what factors, for planning purposes, are you considering to be true?

40. Customer benefits: what customer requirements does this Data Access project address?

1.2 Stakeholder Register: Data Access

41. Is your organization ready for change?

42. How will reports be created?

43. Who is managing stakeholder engagement?

44. What & Why?

45. What are the major Data Access project milestones requiring communications or providing communications opportunities?

46. What is the power of the stakeholder?

47. Who wants to talk about Security?

48. How big is the gap?

49. How should employers make voices heard?

50. What opportunities exist to provide communications?

51. Who are the stakeholders?

52. How much influence do they have on the Data Access project?

1.3 Stakeholder Analysis Matrix: Data Access

53. Identify the stakeholders levels most frequently used –or at least sought– in your Data Access projects and for which purpose?

54. Who will be affected by the work?

55. Guiding question: who shall you involve in the making of the stakeholder map?

56. What is relationship with the Data Access project?

57. What are the mechanisms of public and social accountability, and how can they be made better?

58. What obstacles does your organization face?

59. Are the required specifications for products or services changing?

60. What tools would help you communicate?

61. How to measure the achievement of the Immediate Objective?

62. Who will be affected by the Data Access project?

63. How to measure the achievement of the Outputs?

64. Marketing - reach, distribution, awareness?

65. How to measure the achievement of the Development Objective?

66. Competitor intentions - various?

67. What is the stakeholders name, what is function?

68. Who influences whom?

69. Resources, assets, people?

70. Reputation, presence and reach?

71. Experience, knowledge, data?

2.0 Planning Process Group: Data Access

72. Contingency planning. if a risk event occurs, what will you do?

73. Is the identification of the problems, inequalities and gaps, with respective causes, clear in the Data Access project?

74. What factors are contributing to progress or delay in the achievement of products and results?

75. To what extent and in what ways are the Data Access project contributing to progress towards organizational reform?

76. If a risk event occurs, what will you do?

77. Do the partners have sufficient financial capacity to keep up the benefits produced by the programme?

78. What is the critical path for this Data Access project, and what is the duration of the critical path?

79. To what extent have the target population and participants made the activities own, taking an active role in it?

80. What type of estimation method are you using?

81. How can you make your needs known?

82. In what way has the program contributed towards the issue culture and development included on the public agenda?

83. The Data Access project charter is created in which Data Access project management process group?

84. Is the Data Access project supported by national and/or local organizations?

85. To what extent are the visions and actions of the partners consistent or divergent with regard to the program?

86. What is involved in Data Access project scope management, and why is good Data Access project scope management so important on information technology Data Access projects?

87. Is the Data Access project making progress in helping to achieve the set results?

88. What makes your Data Access project successful?

89. Have operating capacities been created and/or reinforced in partners?

90. When will the Data Access project be done?

2.1 Project Management Plan: Data Access

91. How do you manage time?

92. Are the proposed Data Access project purposes different than a previously authorized Data Access project?

93. Is the budget realistic?

94. How well are you able to manage your risk?

95. Will you add a schedule and diagram?

96. What is risk management?

97. What are the constraints?

98. Are there any windfall benefits that would accrue to the Data Access project sponsor or other parties?

99. What is Data Access project scope management?

100. What is the business need?

101. How can you best help your organization to develop consistent practices in Data Access project management planning stages?

102. Is there an incremental analysis/cost effectiveness analysis of proposed mitigation features based on an approved method and using an accepted

model?

103. What happened during the process that you found interesting?

104. Is mitigation authorized or recommended?

105. What data/reports/tools/etc. do your PMs need?

106. Do there need to be organizational changes?

107. If the Data Access project is complex or scope is specialized, do you have appropriate and/or qualified staff available to perform the tasks?

108. What is the justification?

109. Is the appropriate plan selected based on your organizations objectives and evaluation criteria expressed in Principles and Guidelines policies?

2.2 Scope Management Plan: Data Access

110. What are the risks that could significantly affect procuring consultant staff for the Data Access project?

111. What should you drop in order to add something new?

112. What are the acceptance criteria (process and criteria to be met for key stakeholder acceptance) and who is authorized to sign off?

113. Is there a scope management plan that includes how Data Access project scope will be defined, developed, monitored, validated and controlled?

114. Has a resource management plan been created?

115. Deliverables -are the deliverables tangible and verifiable?

116. Are corrective actions taken when actual results are substantially different from detailed Data Access project plan (variances)?

117. Is there a Steering Committee in place?

118. Are schedule deliverables actually delivered?

119. Are the payment terms being followed?

120. Has the scope management document been

updated and distributed to help prevent scope creep?

121. Can the Data Access project team do several activities in parallel?

122. Is the Data Access project sponsor clearly communicating the business case or rationale for why this Data Access project is needed?

123. What are the risks that could significantly affect the communication on the Data Access project?

124. Has a Data Access project Communications Plan been developed?

125. Is it possible to track all classes of Data Access project work (e.g. scheduled, un-scheduled, defect repair, etc.)?

126. Are measurements and feedback mechanisms incorporated in tracking work effort & refining work estimating techniques?

127. Organizational unit (e.g., department, team, or person) who will accept responsibility for satisfactory completion of the item?

128. What does the critical path really mean?

2.3 Requirements Management Plan: Data Access

129. Describe the process for rejecting the Data Access project requirements. Who has the authority to reject Data Access project requirements?

130. Is requirements work dependent on any other specific Data Access project or non-Data Access project activities (e.g. funding, approvals, procurement)?

131. Do you know which stakeholders will participate in the requirements effort?

132. Is the change control process documented?

133. Does the Data Access project have a Change Control process?

134. How knowledgeable is the primary Stakeholder(s) in the proposed application area?

135. Will the contractors involved take full responsibility?

136. Do you expect stakeholders to be cooperative?

137. Is any organizational data being used or stored?

138. Who is responsible for monitoring and tracking the Data Access project requirements?

139. Will you have access to stakeholders when you need them?

140. How often will the reporting occur?

141. How will bidders price evaluations be done, by deliverables, phases, or in a big bang?

142. Subject to change control?

143. How will the requirements become prioritized?

144. Do you have an appropriate arrangement for meetings?

145. The wbs is developed as part of a joint planning session. and how do you know that youhave done this right?

146. Who will initially review the Data Access project work or products to ensure it meets the applicable acceptance criteria?

147. What went wrong?

148. Is there formal agreement on who has authority to request a change in requirements?

2.4 Requirements Documentation: Data Access

149. How linear / iterative is your Requirements Gathering process (or will it be)?

150. How does what is being described meet the business need?

151. What is effective documentation?

152. Are there legal issues?

153. Is your business case still valid?

154. How can you document system requirements?

155. What is a show stopper in the requirements?

156. What is the risk associated with cost and schedule?

157. What are current process problems?

158. Is new technology needed?

159. What variations exist for a process?

160. Can the requirements be checked?

161. How does the proposed Data Access project contribute to the overall objectives of your organization?

162. How much does requirements engineering cost?

163. How do you get the user to tell you what they want?

164. Has requirements gathering uncovered information that would necessitate changes?

165. What kind of entity is a problem ?

166. Validity. does the system provide the functions which best support the customers needs?

167. What marketing channels do you want to use: e-mail, letter or sms?

168. Does the system provide the functions which best support the customers needs?

2.5 Requirements Traceability Matrix: Data Access

169. Why do you manage scope?

170. How small is small enough?

171. Do you have a clear understanding of all subcontracts in place?

172. Will you use a Requirements Traceability Matrix?

173. How will it affect the stakeholders personally in career?

174. Is there a requirements traceability process in place?

175. What are the chronologies, contingencies, consequences, criteria?

176. What percentage of Data Access projects are producing traceability matrices between requirements and other work products?

177. What is the WBS?

178. Describe the process for approving requirements so they can be added to the traceability matrix and Data Access project work can be performed. Will the Data Access project requirements become approved in writing?

179. How do you manage scope?

180. Why use a WBS?

2.6 Project Scope Statement: Data Access

181. Has everyone approved the Data Access projects scope statement?

182. Are the meetings set up to have assigned note takers that will add action/issues to the issue list?

183. Is your organization structure appropriate for the Data Access projects size and complexity?

184. Is there an information system for the Data Access project?

185. Is the quality function identified and assigned?

186. Do you anticipate new stakeholders joining the Data Access project over time?

187. What actions will be taken to mitigate the risk?

188. What process would you recommend for creating the Data Access project scope statement?

189. Are there completion/verification criteria defined for each task producing an output?

190. Is there a Change Management Board?

191. What is the most common tool for helping define the detail?

192. Are there adequate Data Access project control systems?

193. Will there be a Change Control Process in place?

194. Does the scope statement still need some clarity?

195. Will statistics related to QA be collected, trends analyzed, and problems raised as issues?

196. Will an issue form be in use?

197. Elements of scope management that deal with concept development ?

2.7 Assumption and Constraint Log: Data Access

198. What strengths do you have?

199. What is positive about the current process?

200. How relevant is this attribute to this Data Access project or audit?

201. Has a Data Access project Communications Plan been developed?

202. Contradictory information between different documents?

203. What worked well?

204. Is this process still needed?

205. Diagrams and tables are included to account for complex concepts and increase overall readability?

206. Does the document/deliverable meet all requirements (for example, statement of work) specific to this deliverable?

207. Does the traceability documentation describe the tool and/or mechanism to be used to capture traceability throughout the life cycle?

208. Are there processes in place to ensure internal consistency between the source code components?

209. Do you know what your customers expectations are regarding this process?

210. Are funding and staffing resource estimates sufficiently detailed and documented for use in planning and tracking the Data Access project?

211. Can you perform this task or activity in a more effective manner?

212. Is this model reasonable?

213. Model-building: what data-analytic strategies are useful when building proportional-hazards models?

214. Is the process working, and people are not executing in compliance of the process?

215. How can constraints be violated?

216. Was the document/deliverable developed per the appropriate or required standards (for example, Institute of Electrical and Electronics Engineers standards)?

217. Are there nonconformance issues?

2.8 Work Breakdown Structure: Data Access

218. Where does it take place?

219. When would you develop a Work Breakdown Structure?

220. How much detail?

221. How big is a work-package?

222. When does it have to be done?

223. Why is it useful?

224. Can you make it?

225. How many levels?

226. Do you need another level?

227. What is the probability that the Data Access project duration will exceed xx weeks?

228. Is it a change in scope?

229. Is it still viable?

230. How far down?

231. When do you stop?

232. What has to be done?

233. Who has to do it?

2.9 WBS Dictionary: Data Access

234. Is data disseminated to the contractors management timely, accurate, and usable?

235. Are all affected work authorizations, budgeting, and scheduling documents amended to properly reflect the effects of authorized changes?

236. Does the contractors system identify work accomplishment against the schedule plan?

237. Is subcontracted work defined and identified to the appropriate subcontractor within the proper WBS element?

238. Does the contractors system provide unit or lot costs when applicable?

239. Are current work performance indicators and goals relatable to original goals as modified by contractual changes, replanning, and reprogramming actions?

240. Changes in the nature of the overhead requirements?

241. Does the contractors system provide unit costs, equivalent unit or lot costs in terms of labor, material, other direct, and indirect costs?

242. Major functional areas of contract effort?

243. Software specification, development, integration,

and testing, licenses ?

244. Do the lines of authority for incurring indirect costs correspond to the lines of responsibility for management control of the same components of costs?

245. Is authorization of budgets in excess of the contract budget base controlled formally and done with the full knowledge and recognition of the procuring activity?

246. Are work packages assigned to performing organizations?

247. Are indirect costs charged to the appropriate indirect pools and incurring organization?

248. Is undistributed budget limited to contract effort which cannot yet be planned to CWBS elements at or below the level specified for reporting to the Government?

249. Does the contractor use objective results, design reviews and tests to trace schedule performance?

250. Detailed schedules which support control account and work package start and completion dates/events?

251. Budgets assigned to control accounts?

252. Appropriate work authorization documents which subdivide the contractual effort and responsibilities, within functional organizations?

253. Contractor financial periods; for example, annual?

2.10 Schedule Management Plan: Data Access

254. Are scheduled deliverables actually delivered?

255. Staffing Requirements?

256. Is the critical path valid?

257. Are all resource assumptions documented?

258. Are risk triggers captured?

259. Sensitivity analysis?

260. Does the business case include how the Data Access project aligns with your organizations strategic goals & objectives?

261. What date will the task finish?

262. How does the proposed individual meet each requirement?

263. Does the ims reflect accurate current status and credible start/finish forecasts for all to-go tasks and milestones?

264. Is the plan consistent with industry best practices?

265. Have adequate resources been provided by management to ensure Data Access project success?

266. Have the key elements of a coherent Data Access project management strategy been established?

267. Are adequate resources provided for the quality assurance function?

268. Are the results of quality assurance reviews provided to affected groups & individuals?

269. Are post milestone Data Access project reviews (PMPR) conducted with your organization at least once a year?

270. Does a documented Data Access project organizational policy & plan (i.e. governance model) exist?

271. Has a sponsor been identified?

272. Are all activities captured and do they address all approved work scope in the Data Access project baseline?

2.11 Activity List: Data Access

273. What is the total time required to complete the Data Access project if no delays occur?

274. Should you include sub-activities?

275. Who will perform the work?

276. For other activities, how much delay can be tolerated?

277. Can you determine the activity that must finish, before this activity can start?

278. How difficult will it be to do specific activities on this Data Access project?

279. What are the critical bottleneck activities?

280. How should ongoing costs be monitored to try to keep the Data Access project within budget?

281. What are you counting on?

282. What went right?

283. What went well?

284. How can the Data Access project be displayed graphically to better visualize the activities?

285. In what sequence?

286. Is there anything planned that does not need to be here?

287. What is your organizations history in doing similar activities?

288. What did not go as well?

289. How much slack is available in the Data Access project?

290. Are the required resources available or need to be acquired?

291. What is the probability the Data Access project can be completed in xx weeks?

2.12 Activity Attributes: Data Access

292. How many resources do you need to complete the work scope within a limit of X number of days?

293. How many days do you need to complete the work scope with a limit of X number of resources?

294. Activity: what is Missing?

295. Do you feel very comfortable with your prediction?

296. Have you identified the Activity Leveling Priority code value on each activity?

297. What conclusions/generalizations can you draw from this?

298. Can more resources be added?

299. Can you re-assign any activities to another resource to resolve an over-allocation?

300. Have constraints been applied to the start and finish milestones for the phases?

301. Would you consider either of corresponding activities an outlier?

302. Where else does it apply?

303. How else could the items be grouped?

304. What activity do you think you should spend the most time on?

305. How difficult will it be to complete specific activities on this Data Access project?

306. Why?

307. Does your organization of the data change its meaning?

2.13 Milestone List: Data Access

308. Which path is the critical path?

309. Obstacles faced?

310. Do you foresee any technical risks or developmental challenges?

311. Loss of key staff?

312. Vital contracts and partners?

313. Can you derive how soon can the whole Data Access project finish?

314. Continuity, supply chain robustness?

315. How late can the activity start?

316. What would happen if a delivery of material was one week late?

317. Competitive advantages?

318. Who will manage the Data Access project on a day-to-day basis?

319. How will the milestone be verified?

320. Environmental effects?

321. Level of the Innovation?

322. Insurmountable weaknesses?

323. What has been done so far?

324. Timescales, deadlines and pressures?

325. How late can each activity be finished and started?

2.14 Network Diagram: Data Access

326. What are the Major Administrative Issues?

327. If x is long, what would be the completion time if you break x into two parallel parts of y weeks and z weeks?

328. If the Data Access project network diagram cannot change and you have extra personnel resources, what is the BEST thing to do?

329. What job or jobs could run concurrently?

330. What are the tools?

331. Why must you schedule milestones, such as reviews, throughout the Data Access project?

332. Where do you schedule uncertainty time?

333. What to do and When?

334. Exercise: what is the probability that the Data Access project duration will exceed xx weeks?

335. Will crashing x weeks return more in benefits than it costs?

336. If a current contract exists, can you provide the vendor name, contract start, and contract expiration date?

337. What is the completion time?

338. Planning: who, how long, what to do?

339. What controls the start and finish of a job?

340. Are the gantt chart and/or network diagram updated periodically and used to assess the overall Data Access project timetable?

341. What job or jobs precede it?

342. How confident can you be in your milestone dates and the delivery date?

343. Where do schedules come from?

344. What activities must follow this activity?

345. Are the required resources available?

2.15 Activity Resource Requirements: Data Access

346. What are constraints that you might find during the Human Resource Planning process?

347. When does monitoring begin?

348. Anything else?

349. How do you handle petty cash?

350. How many signatures do you require on a check and does this match what is in your policy and procedures?

351. Organizational Applicability?

352. Other support in specific areas?

353. Which logical relationship does the PDM use most often?

354. Do you use tools like decomposition and rolling-wave planning to produce the activity list and other outputs?

355. What is the Work Plan Standard?

356. Time for overtime?

357. Are there unresolved issues that need to be addressed?

358. Why do you do that?

2.16 Resource Breakdown Structure: Data Access

359. Why do you do it?

360. Why time management?

361. What defines a successful Data Access project?

362. Which resource planning tool provides information on resource responsibility and accountability?

363. Who will be used as a Data Access project team member?

364. When do they need the information?

365. Why is this important?

366. Any changes from stakeholders?

367. How should the information be delivered?

368. Who is allowed to perform which functions?

369. What is the number one predictor of a groups productivity?

370. How can this help you with team building?

371. Who will use the system?

372. What is Data Access project communication management?

373. How difficult will it be to do specific activities on this Data Access project?

2.17 Activity Duration Estimates: Data Access

374. Is a contract developed which obligates the seller and the buyer?

375. Are processes defined to monitor Data Access project cost and schedule variances?

376. Does the case present a realistic scenario?

377. Will the new application negatively affect the current IT infrastructure?

378. What time management activity should you do NEXT?

379. What are the main types of goods and services being outsourced?

380. Are the causes of all variances identified?

381. Describe a Data Access project that suffered from scope creep. Could it have been avoided?

382. Which frame seemed to be the most important and why?

383. What are the Data Access project management deliverables of each process group?

384. How can organizations use a weighted decision matrix to evaluate proposals as part of source

selection?

385. Is evaluation criteria defined to rate proposals?

386. On which process should team members spend the most time?

387. Why is activity definition the first process involved in Data Access project time management?

388. Which type of mathematical analysis is being used?

389. Does a process exist to determine which risk events to accept and which events to disregard?

390. What should be done NEXT?

391. What are the main types of contracts if you do decide to outsource?

392. Is the cost performance monitored to identify variances from the plan?

393. Will it help promote wellness at your organization and reduce insurance costs?

2.18 Duration Estimating Worksheet: Data Access

394. Will the Data Access project collaborate with the local community and leverage resources?

395. How should ongoing costs be monitored to try to keep the Data Access project within budget?

396. When, then?

397. When does your organization expect to be able to complete it?

398. Why estimate costs?

399. Is this operation cost effective?

400. Value pocket identification & quantification what are value pockets?

401. What is your role?

402. Done before proceeding with this activity or what can be done concurrently?

403. Is a construction detail attached (to aid in explanation)?

404. What is an Average Data Access project?

405. Small or large Data Access project?

406. What work will be included in the Data Access project?

407. Do any colleagues have experience with your organization and/or RFPs?

408. What is next?

409. Define the work as completely as possible. What work will be included in the Data Access project?

410. What questions do you have?

2.19 Project Schedule: Data Access

411. What is risk?

412. How do you use schedules?

413. Understand the constraints used in preparing the schedule. Are activities connected because logic dictates the order in which others occur?

414. Did the final product meet or exceed user expectations?

415. Is infrastructure setup part of your Data Access project?

416. How closely did the initial Data Access project Schedule compare with the actual schedule?

417. How can you address that situation?

418. Month Data Access project take?

419. Did the Data Access project come in on schedule?

420. Is there a Schedule Management Plan that establishes the criteria and activities for developing, monitoring and controlling the Data Access project schedule?

421. Schedule/cost recovery?

422. How effectively were issues able to be resolved

without impacting the Data Access project Schedule or Budget?

423. Have all Data Access project delays been adequately accounted for, communicated to all stakeholders and adjustments made in overall Data Access project schedule?

424. Are quality inspections and review activities listed in the Data Access project schedule(s)?

425. If there are any qualifying green components to this Data Access project, what portion of the total Data Access project cost is green?

426. Are the original Data Access project schedule and budget realistic?

427. What is the difference?

428. How can you fix it?

429. Why is this particularly bad?

2.20 Cost Management Plan: Data Access

430. Are all vendor contracts closed out?

431. Are mitigation strategies identified?

432. Is current scope of the Data Access project substantially different than that originally defined?

433. Is the steering committee active in Data Access project oversight?

434. Are all payments made according to the contract(s)?

435. Does the Data Access project have a Quality Culture?

436. Are the key elements of a Data Access project Charter present?

437. Has the budget been baselined?

438. Have key stakeholders been identified?

439. Risk rating?

440. Is the Data Access project schedule available for all Data Access project team members to review?

441. Are procurement deliverables arriving on time and to specification?

442. Are status reports received per the Data Access project Plan?

443. Is an industry recognized mechanized support tool(s) being used for Data Access project scheduling & tracking?

444. Are meeting minutes captured and sent out after the meeting?

445. Is there an issues management plan in place?

446. Does the detailed work plan match the complexity of tasks with the capabilities of personnel?

447. Are vendor contract reports, reviews and visits conducted periodically?

2.21 Activity Cost Estimates: Data Access

448. Were decisions made in a timely manner?

449. Does the activity use a common approach or business function to deliver its results?

450. How Award?

451. Based on your Data Access project communication management plan, what worked well?

452. What were things that you need to improve?

453. Can you change your activities?

454. Does the estimator have experience?

455. What procedures are put in place regarding bidding and cost comparisons, if any?

456. What makes a good activity description?

457. Who & what determines the need for contracted services?

458. Will you need to provide essential services information about activities?

459. What is the activity recast of the budget?

460. How and when do you enter into Data Access project Procurement Management?

461. Can you delete activities or make them inactive?

462. How do you change activities?

463. What is procurement?

464. What happens if you cannot produce the documentation for the single audit?

465. How many activities should you have?

2.22 Cost Estimating Worksheet: Data Access

466. How will the results be shared and to whom?

467. What costs are to be estimated?

468. Will the Data Access project collaborate with the local community and leverage resources?

469. Does the Data Access project provide innovative ways for stakeholders to overcome obstacles or deliver better outcomes?

470. Can a trend be established from historical performance data on the selected measure and are the criteria for using trend analysis or forecasting methods met?

471. What happens to any remaining funds not used?

472. Identify the timeframe necessary to monitor progress and collect data to determine how the selected measure has changed?

473. What info is needed?

474. Ask: are others positioned to know, are others credible, and will others cooperate?

475. What is the estimated labor cost today based upon this information?

476. Who is best positioned to know and assist in identifying corresponding factors?

477. What is the purpose of estimating?

478. What will others want?

479. What can be included?

480. Is it feasible to establish a control group arrangement?

481. What additional Data Access project(s) could be initiated as a result of this Data Access project?

482. Is the Data Access project responsive to community need?

2.23 Cost Baseline: Data Access

483. What is cost and Data Access project cost management?

484. How do you manage cost?

485. Has operations management formally accepted responsibility for operating and maintaining the product(s) or service(s) delivered by the Data Access project?

486. Have all approved changes to the Data Access project requirement been identified and impact on the performance, cost, and schedule baselines documented?

487. What do you want to measure ?

488. Data Access project goals -should others be reconsidered?

489. Has the documentation relating to operation and maintenance of the product(s) or service(s) been delivered to, and accepted by, operations management?

490. For what purpose ?

491. How fast?

492. Definition of done can be traced back to the definitions of what are you providing to the customer in terms of deliverables?

493. What is your organizations history in doing similar tasks?

494. Is there anything unique in this Data Access projects scope statement that will affect resources?

495. Have all the product or service deliverables been accepted by the customer?

496. Have you identified skills that are missing from your team?

497. Does the suggested change request seem to represent a necessary enhancement to the product?

498. Are procedures defined by which the cost baseline may be changed?

499. What would the life cycle costs be?

500. What is it ?

501. Are you meeting with your team regularly?

502. Is the requested change request a result of changes in other Data Access project(s)?

2.24 Quality Management Plan: Data Access

503. Was trending evident between reviews?

504. How do senior leaders create an environment that encourages learning and innovation?

505. How do you measure?

506. Was trending evident between audits?

507. After observing execution of process, is it in compliance with the documented Plan?

508. What are your organizations current levels and trends for the already stated measures related to financial and marketplace performance?

509. How does your organization establish and maintain customer relationships?

510. Does a prospective decision remain the same regardless of what the data show is?

511. How does your organization design processes to ensure others meet customer and others requirements?

512. How is staff trained?

513. Were there any deficiencies / issues in prior years self-assessment?

514. Checking the completeness and appropriateness of the sampling and testing. Were the right locations/samples tested for the right parameters?

515. How do you ensure that your sampling methods and procedures meet your data quality objectives?

516. How does your organization make it easy for customers to seek assistance or complain?

517. How does your organization determine the requirements and product/service features important to customers?

518. Have Data Access project management standards and procedures been established and documented?

519. Are you meeting the quality standards?

520. Is there a Quality Management Plan?

521. What are you trying to accomplish?

522. What is the Difference Between a QMP and QAPP?

2.25 Quality Metrics: Data Access

523. Can you correlate your quality metrics to profitability?

524. Have risk areas been identified?

525. How is it being measured?

526. Who is willing to lead?

527. What are your organizations next steps?

528. Was material distributed on time?

529. Should a modifier be included?

530. What group is empowered to define quality requirements?

531. Has risk analysis been adequately reviewed?

532. What approved evidence based screening tools can be used?

533. Do you stratify metrics by product or site?

534. Can visual measures help you to filter visualizations of interest?

535. Is the reporting frequency appropriate?

536. How exactly do you define when differences exist?

537. Are documents on hand to provide explanations of privacy and confidentiality?

538. Are there already quality metrics available that detect nonlinear embeddings and trends similar to the users perception?

539. Does risk analysis documentation meet standards?

540. What does this tell us?

541. Subjective quality component: customer satisfaction, how do you measure it?

2.26 Process Improvement Plan: Data Access

542. What personnel are the change agents for your initiative?

543. Have the supporting tools been developed or acquired?

544. Are you making progress on your improvement plan?

545. What personnel are the champions for the initiative?

546. What is quality and how will you ensure it?

547. Are there forms and procedures to collect and record the data?

548. Does your process ensure quality?

549. Are you making progress on the goals?

550. Who should prepare the process improvement action plan?

551. What personnel are the coaches for your initiative?

552. What personnel are the sponsors for that initiative?

553. If a process improvement framework is being used, which elements will help the problems and goals listed?

554. Have storage and access mechanisms and procedures been determined?

555. Everyone agrees on what process improvement is, right?

556. To elicit goal statements, do you ask a question such as, What do you want to achieve?

557. What lessons have you learned so far?

558. What actions are needed to address the problems and achieve the goals?

559. Why quality management?

2.27 Responsibility Assignment Matrix: Data Access

560. How do you assist them to be as productive as possible?

561. All cwbs elements specified for external reporting?

562. Does each activity-deliverable have exactly one Accountable responsibility, so that accountability is clear and decisions can be made quickly?

563. The total budget for the contract (including estimates for authorized and unpriced work)?

564. Are all elements of indirect expense identified to overhead cost budgets of Data Access projections?

565. With too many people labeled as doing the work, are there too many hands involved?

566. How do you manage remotely to staff in other Divisions?

567. Are your organizations and items of cost assigned to each pool identified?

568. Contemplated overhead expenditure for each period based on the best information currently available?

569. Cwbs elements to be subcontracted, with

identification of subcontractors?

570. How many people do you need?

571. What can you do to improve productivity?

572. Are control accounts opened and closed based on the start and completion of work contained therein?

573. Is work progressively subdivided into detailed work packages as requirements are defined?

574. Is it safe to say you can handle more work or that some tasks you are supposed to do arent worth doing?

575. How do you manage human resources?

576. Are overhead costs budgets established on a basis consistent with anticipated direct business base?

2.28 Roles and Responsibilities: Data Access

577. What specific behaviors did you observe?

578. What should you do now to ensure that you are exceeding expectations and excelling in your current position?

579. Once the responsibilities are defined for the Data Access project, have the deliverables, roles and responsibilities been clearly communicated to every participant?

580. Are Data Access project team roles and responsibilities identified and documented?

581. Have you ever been a part of this team?

582. What is working well within your organizations performance management system?

583. Is the data complete?

584. What areas of supervision are challenging for you?

585. Are the quality assurance functions and related roles and responsibilities clearly defined?

586. Key conclusions and recommendations: Are conclusions and recommendations relevant and acceptable?

587. Who is responsible for implementation activities and where will the functions, roles and responsibilities be defined?

588. Are Data Access project team roles and responsibilities identified and documented?

589. What is working well?

590. What expectations were met?

591. Influence: what areas of organizational decision making are you able to influence when you do not have authority to make the final decision?

592. Who: who is involved?

593. What should you do now to prepare yourself for a promotion, increased responsibilities or a different job?

594. What should you do now to prepare for your career 5+ years from now?

595. Authority: what areas/Data Access projects in your work do you have the authority to decide upon and act on the already stated decisions?

2.29 Human Resource Management Plan: Data Access

596. Is there a formal set of procedures supporting Issues Management?

597. How well does your organization communicate?

598. Are changes in deliverable commitments agreed to by all affected groups & individuals?

599. Have all team members been part of identifying risks?

600. Are written status reports provided on a designated frequent basis?

601. Are there checklists created to determine if all quality processes are followed?

602. Are estimating assumptions and constraints captured?

603. Identify who is needed on the core Data Access project team to complete Data Access project deliverables and achieve its goals and objectives. What skills, knowledge and experiences are required?

604. Are enough systems & user personnel assigned to the Data Access project?

605. How do you determine what key skills and talents are needed to meet the objectives. Is your

organization primarily focused on a specific industry?

606. Account for the purpose of this Data Access project by describing, at a high-level, what will be done. What is this Data Access project aiming to achieve?

607. What skills, knowledge and experiences are required?

608. Have the key functions and capabilities been defined and assigned to each release or iteration?

609. Was the Data Access project schedule reviewed by all stakeholders and formally accepted?

610. Is quality monitored from the perspective of the customers needs and expectations?

611. Are status reports received per the Data Access project Plan?

612. Do Data Access project teams & team members report on status / activities / progress?

613. Has the schedule been baselined?

2.30 Communications Management Plan: Data Access

614. Do you feel a register helps?

615. Who is responsible?

616. What is the stakeholders level of authority?

617. Who is the stakeholder?

618. Will messages be directly related to the release strategy or phases of the Data Access project?

619. Where do team members get information?

620. What does the stakeholder need from the team?

621. What communications method?

622. Who are the members of the governing body?

623. What are the interrelationships?

624. How did the term stakeholder originate?

625. Are stakeholders internal or external?

626. What steps can you take for a positive relationship?

627. Why is stakeholder engagement important?

628. How will the person responsible for executing the communication item be notified?

629. Who did you turn to if you had questions?

630. What approaches to you feel are the best ones to use?

631. Is the stakeholder role recognized by your organization?

632. Are you constantly rushing from meeting to meeting?

2.31 Risk Management Plan: Data Access

633. Is the customer willing to establish rapid communication links with the developer?

634. Are there alternative opinions/solutions/ processes you should explore?

635. Should the risk be taken at all?

636. What should be done with non-critical risks?

637. What are the cost, schedule and resource impacts if the risk does occur?

638. Financial risk: can your organization afford to undertake the Data Access project?

639. Is the customer willing to commit significant time to the requirements gathering process?

640. Is the number of people on the Data Access project team adequate to do the job?

641. Who/what can assist?

642. What are it-specific requirements?

643. Do you have a mechanism for managing change?

644. Minimize cost and financial risk?

645. Is there additional information that would make you more confident about your analysis?

646. Is Data Access project scope stable?

647. Do requirements demand the use of new analysis, design, or testing methods?

648. What other risks are created by choosing an avoidance strategy?

649. How will the Data Access project know if your organizations risk response actions were effective?

650. Are the reports useful and easy to read?

651. Which risks should get the attention?

2.32 Risk Register: Data Access

652. Severity Prediction?

653. Who is accountable?

654. Are implemented controls working as others should?

655. Preventative actions - planned actions to reduce the likelihood a risk will occur and/or reduce the seriousness should it occur. What should you do now?

656. Which key risks have ineffective responses or outstanding improvement actions?

657. Is further information required before making a decision?

658. What has changed since the last period?

659. Methodology: how will risk management be performed on this Data Access project?

660. What are the main aims, objectives of the policy, strategy, or service and the intended outcomes?

661. How could corresponding Risk affect the Data Access project in terms of cost and schedule?

662. When will it happen?

663. Are corrective measures implemented as planned?

664. What will be done?

665. Cost/benefit – how much will the proposed mitigations cost and how does this cost compare with the potential cost of the risk event/situation should it occur?

666. How well are risks controlled?

667. Are there other alternative controls that could be implemented?

668. What are the assumptions and current status that support the assessment of the risk?

669. Amongst the action plans and recommendations that you have to introduce are there some that could stop or delay the overall program?

670. What is the probability and impact of the risk occurring?

2.33 Probability and Impact Assessment: Data Access

671. What are the preparations required for facing difficulties?

672. How do you maximize short-term return on investment?

673. Have customers been involved fully in the definition of requirements?

674. Are testing tools available and suitable?

675. What are the tools and techniques used in managing the challenges faced?

676. What risks does the employee encounter?

677. Is security a central objective?

678. Have top software and customer managers formally committed to support the Data Access project?

679. Can you avoid altogether some things that might go wrong?

680. How completely has the customer been identified?

681. Are formal technical reviews part of this process?

682. Who should be responsible for the monitoring and tracking of the indicators youhave identified?

683. Is the process supported by tools?

684. What will be the environmental impact of the Data Access project?

685. How will economic events and trends likely affect the Data Access project?

686. Risks should be identified during which phase of Data Access project management life cycle?

687. How do risks change during the Data Access projects life cycle?

688. What are the likely future requirements?

689. Are flexibility and reuse paramount?

690. What are the current requirements of the customer?

2.34 Probability and Impact Matrix: Data Access

691. Are the best people available?

692. What are the current demands of the customer?

693. Sensitivity analysis -which risks will have the most impact on the Data Access project?

694. Economic to take on the Data Access project?

695. Are the software tools integrated with each other?

696. Do you manage the process through use of metrics?

697. How do you analyze the risks in the different types of Data Access projects?

698. What should you do FIRST?

699. What are the ways you measure and evaluate risks?

700. What are the chances the event will occur?

701. Are you working on the right risks?

702. What is the likelihood of a breakthrough?

703. Are you on schedule?

704. Which of your Data Access projects should be selected when compared with other Data Access projects?

705. Amount of reused software?

2.35 Risk Data Sheet: Data Access

706. Potential for recurrence?

707. What can happen?

708. If it happens, what are the consequences?

709. What will be the consequences if it happens?

710. What actions can be taken to eliminate or remove risk?

711. What if client refuses?

712. Whom do you serve (customers)?

713. What are you here for (Mission)?

714. Who has a vested interest in how you perform as your organization (our stakeholders)?

715. Do effective diagnostic tests exist?

716. Has a sensitivity analysis been carried out?

717. What is the environment within which you operate (social trends, economic, community values, broad based participation, national directions etc.)?

718. What are you trying to achieve (Objectives)?

719. How can hazards be reduced?

720. What do you know?

721. What is the chance that it will happen?

722. What do people affected think about the need for, and practicality of preventive measures?

723. How reliable is the data source?

2.36 Procurement Management Plan: Data Access

724. Are the people assigned to the Data Access project sufficiently qualified?

725. Is stakeholder involvement adequate?

726. Are Data Access project leaders committed to this Data Access project full time?

727. Are actuals compared against estimates to analyze and correct variances?

728. Has the Data Access project scope been baselined?

729. Are quality metrics defined?

730. Have all necessary approvals been obtained?

731. Is it standard practice to formally commit stakeholders to the Data Access project via agreements?

732. Are assumptions being identified, recorded, analyzed, qualified and closed?

733. In which phase of the Acquisition Process Cycle does source qualifications reside?

734. Is a payment system in place with proper reviews and approvals?

735. Are the Data Access project team members located locally to the users/stakeholders?

736. Is Data Access project status reviewed with the steering and executive teams at appropriate intervals?

737. Are issues raised, assessed, actioned, and resolved in a timely and efficient manner?

738. Similar Data Access projects?

739. Are changes in scope (deliverable commitments) agreed to by all affected groups & individuals?

740. Is there an approved case?

741. What are your quality assurance overheads?

2.37 Source Selection Criteria: Data Access

742. Team leads: what is your process for assigning ratings?

743. Will the technical evaluation factor unnecessarily force the acquisition into a higher-priced market segment?

744. Does an evaluation need to include the identification of strengths and weaknesses?

745. Is the contracting office likely to receive more purchase requests for this item or service during the coming year?

746. Is a letter of commitment from each proposed team member and key subcontractor included?

747. How is past performance evaluated?

748. How can solicitation Schedules be improved to yield more effective price competition?

749. Are evaluators ready to begin this task?

750. How will you evaluate offerors proposals?

751. What should be the contracting officers strategy?

752. Who is entitled to a debriefing?

753. How much weight should be placed on past performance information?

754. If the costs are normalized, please account for how the normalization is conducted. Is a cost realism analysis used?

755. How should oral presentations be evaluated?

756. What evidence should be provided regarding proposal evaluations?

757. Does your documentation identify why the team concurs or differs with reported performance from past performance report (CPARs, questionnaire responses, etc.)?

758. How do you facilitate evaluation against published criteria?

759. Does the evaluation of any change include an impact analysis; how will the change affect the scope, time, cost, and quality of the goods or services being provided?

760. Is a cost realism analysis used?

2.38 Stakeholder Management Plan: Data Access

761. Are communication systems proposed compatible with staff skills and experience?

762. Are target dates established for each milestone deliverable?

763. Do Data Access project managers participating in the Data Access project know the Data Access projects true status first hand?

764. Is the current scope of the Data Access project substantially different than that originally defined?

765. Are internal Data Access project status meetings held at reasonable intervals?

766. Are metrics used to evaluate and manage Vendors?

767. Is Data Access project status reviewed with the steering and executive teams at appropriate intervals?

768. Are there cosmetic errors that hinder readability and comprehension?

769. Does the Data Access project have a Quality Culture?

770. Who will perform the review(s)?

771. Is the quality assurance team identified?

772. Does the role of the Data Access project Team cease upon the delivery of the Data Access projects outputs?

773. Have all involved Data Access project stakeholders and work groups committed to the Data Access project?

774. What are the criteria for selecting other suppliers, including subcontractors?

775. How many Data Access project staff does this specific process affect?

776. Have you eliminated all duplicative tasks or manual efforts, where appropriate?

777. How accurate and complete is the information?

2.39 Change Management Plan: Data Access

778. What can you do to minimise misinterpretation and negative perceptions?

779. Has an information & communications plan been developed?

780. Are there any restrictions on who can receive the communications?

781. Will a different work structure focus people on what is important?

782. What is the reason for the communication?

783. Is there support for this application(s) and are the details available for distribution?

784. Has a training need analysis been carried out?

785. What are the training strategies?

786. Who will fund the training?

787. Who in the business it includes?

788. Has the training co-ordinator been provided with the training details and put in place the necessary arrangements?

789. Why would a Data Access project run more

smoothly when change management is emphasized from the beginning?

790. Have the systems been configured and tested?

791. Who is responsible for which tasks?

792. What will be the preferred method of delivery?

793. Will the culture embrace or reject this change?

794. What roles within your organization are affected, and how?

795. Who should be involved in developing a change management strategy?

796. What risks may occur upfront, during implementation and after implementation?

797. Where do you want to be?

3.0 Executing Process Group: Data Access

798. Will additional funds be needed for hardware or software?

799. Will outside resources be needed to help?

800. Just how important is your work to the overall success of the Data Access project?

801. How well defined and documented were the Data Access project management processes you chose to use?

802. Does software appear easy to learn?

803. Do schedule issues conflicts?

804. Mitigate. what will you do to minimize the impact should a risk event occur?

805. What are the main parts of the scope statement?

806. What were things that you did well, and could improve, and how?

807. What are the key components of the Data Access project communications plan?

808. Specific - is the objective clear in terms of what, how, when, and where the situation will be changed?

809. Who are the Data Access project stakeholders?

810. Will new hardware or software be required for servers or client machines?

811. What areas were overlooked on this Data Access project?

812. How can software assist in Data Access project communications?

813. What are crucial elements of successful Data Access project plan execution?

814. What were things that you did very well and want to do the same again on the next Data Access project?

3.1 Team Member Status Report: Data Access

815. The problem with Reward & Recognition Programs is that the truly deserving people all too often get left out. How can you make it practical?

816. What is to be done?

817. Does your organization have the means (staff, money, contract, etc.) to produce or to acquire the product, good, or service?

818. How does this product, good, or service meet the needs of the Data Access project and your organization as a whole?

819. When a teams productivity and success depend on collaboration and the efficient flow of information, what generally fails them?

820. What specific interest groups do you have in place?

821. Are the products of your organizations Data Access projects meeting customers objectives?

822. Is there evidence that staff is taking a more professional approach toward management of your organizations Data Access projects?

823. How it is to be done?

824. Are your organizations Data Access projects more successful over time?

825. Do you have an Enterprise Data Access project Management Office (EPMO)?

826. Will the staff do training or is that done by a third party?

827. How much risk is involved?

828. Why is it to be done?

829. Does the product, good, or service already exist within your organization?

830. Are the attitudes of staff regarding Data Access project work improving?

831. How can you make it practical?

832. Does every department have to have a Data Access project Manager on staff?

833. How will resource planning be done?

3.2 Change Request: Data Access

834. Who will perform the change?

835. What should be regulated in a change control operating instruction?

836. How do team members communicate with each other?

837. How do you get changes (code) out in a timely manner?

838. Who needs to approve change requests?

839. When do you create a change request?

840. Will the change use memory to the extent that other functions will be not have sufficient memory to operate effectively?

841. What type of changes does change control take into account?

842. What must be taken into consideration when introducing change control programs?

843. Where do changes come from?

844. Will there be a change request form in use?

845. What are the requirements for urgent changes?

846. How is quality being addressed on the Data

Access project?

847. Since there are no change requests in your Data Access project at this point, what must you have before you begin?

848. Are there requirements attributes that are strongly related to the complexity and size?

849. What is the relationship between requirements attributes and reliability?

850. Screen shots or attachments included in a Change Request?

851. How fast will change requests be approved?

852. Who has responsibility for approving and ranking changes?

853. Has your address changed?

3.3 Change Log: Data Access

854. Is the submitted change a new change or a modification of a previously approved change?

855. How does this change affect scope?

856. Do the described changes impact on the integrity or security of the system?

857. Who initiated the change request?

858. When was the request submitted?

859. When was the request approved?

860. Is this a mandatory replacement?

861. Is the change request within Data Access project scope?

862. Is the requested change request a result of changes in other Data Access project(s)?

863. Is the change request open, closed or pending?

864. Will the Data Access project fail if the change request is not executed?

865. How does this change affect the timeline of the schedule?

866. Is the change backward compatible without limitations?

867. Should a more thorough impact analysis be conducted?

868. How does this relate to the standards developed for specific business processes?

869. Does the suggested change request represent a desired enhancement to the products functionality?

3.4 Decision Log: Data Access

870. Do strategies and tactics aimed at less than full control reduce the costs of management or simply shift the cost burden?

871. What was the rationale for the decision?

872. At what point in time does loss become unacceptable?

873. What is your overall strategy for quality control / quality assurance procedures?

874. What are the cost implications?

875. Does anything need to be adjusted?

876. Who is the decisionmaker?

877. Adversarial environment. is your opponent open to a non-traditional workflow, or will it likely challenge anything you do?

878. What makes you different or better than others companies selling the same thing?

879. With whom was the decision shared or considered?

880. Is your opponent open to a non-traditional workflow, or will it likely challenge anything you do?

881. Which variables make a critical difference?

882. Meeting purpose; why does this team meet?

883. Decision-making process; how will the team make decisions?

884. How effective is maintaining the log at facilitating organizational learning?

885. How do you define success?

886. How does the use a Decision Support System influence the strategies/tactics or costs?

887. It becomes critical to track and periodically revisit both operational effectiveness; Are you noticing all that you need to, and are you interpreting what you see effectively?

888. What eDiscovery problem or issue did your organization set out to fix or make better?

889. Linked to original objective?

3.5 Quality Audit: Data Access

890. How does the organization know that its system for maintaining and advancing the capabilities of its staff, particularly in relation to the Mission of the organization, is appropriately effective and constructive?

891. How does your organization know that its staff are presenting original work, and properly acknowledging the work of others?

892. How does your organization know that its information technology system is serving its needs as effectively and constructively as is appropriate?

893. Is progress against the intentions measurable?

894. How does your organization know that its policy management system is appropriately effective and constructive?

895. Do prior clients have a positive opinion of your organization?

896. Are the intentions consistent with external obligations (such as applicable laws)?

897. How does your organization know that the support for its staff is appropriately effective and constructive?

898. How does your organization know that its systems for meeting staff extracurricular learning

support requirements are appropriately effective and constructive?

899. How does your organization know whether they are adhering to mission and achieving objectives?

900. Is the reports overall tone appropriate?

901. Are all complaints involving the possible failure of a device, labeling, or packaging to meet any of its specifications reviewed, evaluated, and investigated?

902. Do the suppliers use a formal quality system?

903. Is there a written corporate quality policy?

904. Is quality audit a prerequisite for program accreditation or program recognition?

905. How does your organization know that its management system is appropriately effective and constructive?

906. What mechanisms exist for identification of staff development needs?

907. How does your organization know that its risk management system is appropriately effective and constructive?

908. For each device to be reconditioned, are device specifications, such as appropriate engineering drawings, component specifications and software specifications, maintained?

909. What will the Observer get to Observe?

3.6 Team Directory: Data Access

910. When does information need to be distributed?

911. How do unidentified risks impact the outcome of the Data Access project?

912. Where should the information be distributed?

913. Who will report Data Access project status to all stakeholders?

914. Who will write the meeting minutes and distribute?

915. How will the team handle changes?

916. When will you produce deliverables?

917. Where will the product be used and/or delivered or built when appropriate?

918. Process decisions: are contractors adequately prosecuting the work?

919. Have you decided when to celebrate the Data Access projects completion date?

920. Why is the work necessary?

921. How and in what format should information be presented?

922. Decisions: is the most suitable form of contract

being used?

923. Decisions: what could be done better to improve the quality of the constructed product?

924. What needs to be communicated?

925. Who are the Team Members?

926. Do purchase specifications and configurations match requirements?

927. Days from the time the issue is identified?

3.7 Team Operating Agreement: Data Access

928. Did you recap the meeting purpose, time, and expectations?

929. Do you begin with a question to engage everyone?

930. Methodologies: how will key team processes be implemented, such as training, research, work deliverable production, review and approval processes, knowledge management, and meeting procedures?

931. Do you vary your voice pace, tone and pitch to engage participants and gain involvement?

932. Do team members need to frequently communicate as a full group to make timely decisions?

933. How will you divide work equitably?

934. What are the boundaries (organizational or geographic) within which you operate?

935. Do you prevent individuals from dominating the meeting?

936. What is your unique contribution to your organization?

937. Do you determine the meeting length and time of day?

938. What is culture?

939. How will group handle unplanned absences?

940. Are there more than two native languages represented by your team?

941. Do you send out the agenda and meeting materials in advance?

942. How do you want to be thought of and known within your organization?

943. Are there the right people on your team?

944. Has the appropriate access to relevant data and analysis capability been granted?

945. To whom do you deliver your services?

946. Do you post meeting notes and the recording (if used) and notify participants?

947. Do you call or email participants to ensure understanding, follow-through and commitment to the meeting outcomes?

3.8 Team Performance Assessment: Data Access

948. Can team performance be reliably measured in simulator and live exercises using the same assessment tool?

949. Delaying market entry: how long is too long?

950. What are teams?

951. To what degree will new and supplemental skills be introduced as the need is recognized?

952. Do you promptly inform members about major developments that may affect them?

953. Effects of crew composition on crew performance: Does the whole equal the sum of its parts?

954. To what degree can the team measure progress against specific goals?

955. To what degree are staff involved as partners in the improvement process?

956. To what degree are the goals realistic?

957. To what degree are the relative importance and priority of the goals clear to all team members?

958. How hard do you try to make a good selection?

959. To what degree are the members clear on what they are individually responsible for and what they are jointly responsible for?

960. To what degree can team members meet frequently enough to accomplish the teams ends?

961. How does Data Access project termination impact Data Access project team members?

962. To what degree can the team ensure that all members are individually and jointly accountable for the teams purpose, goals, approach, and work-products?

963. To what degree is there a sense that only the team can succeed?

964. To what degree do members understand and articulate the same purpose without relying on ambiguous abstractions?

965. If you have received criticism from reviewers that your work suffered from method variance, what was the circumstance?

966. To what degree are the goals ambitious?

967. To what degree do team members agree with the goals, relative importance, and the ways in which achievement will be measured?

3.9 Team Member Performance Assessment: Data Access

968. What are they responsible for?

969. How do you implement Cost Reduction?

970. What changes do you need to make to align practices with beliefs?

971. What is collaboration?

972. Which training platform formats (i.e., mobile, virtual, videogame-based) were implemented in your effort(s)?

973. What is the role of the Reviewer?

974. How will you identify your Team Leaders?

975. What specific plans do you have for developing effective cross-platform assessments in a blended learning environment?

976. How accurately is your plan implemented?

977. To what degree do members articulate the goals beyond the team membership?

978. Is it critical or vital to the job?

979. Verify business objectives. Are they appropriate, and well-articulated?

980. How do you use data to inform instruction and improve staff achievement?

981. What are acceptable governance changes?

982. What steps have you taken to improve performance?

983. What is needed for effective data teams?

984. What makes them effective?

985. How do you currently use the time that is available?

3.10 Issue Log: Data Access

986. How is this initiative related to other portfolios, programs, or Data Access projects?

987. Are stakeholder roles recognized by your organization?

988. Is there an important stakeholder who is actively opposed and will not receive messages?

989. Which team member will work with each stakeholder?

990. How often do you engage with stakeholders?

991. Are they needed?

992. Who is involved as you identify stakeholders?

993. Do you have members of your team responsible for certain stakeholders?

994. Do you feel more overwhelmed by stakeholders?

995. What effort will a change need?

996. How were past initiatives successful?

997. Is the issue log kept in a safe place?

998. In your work, how much time is spent on stakeholder identification?

999. Do you often overlook a key stakeholder or stakeholder group?

4.0 Monitoring and Controlling Process Group: Data Access

1000. How to ensure validity, quality and consistency?

1001. How will staff learn how to use the deliverables?

1002. Just how important is your work to the overall success of the Data Access project?

1003. Is the program making progress in helping to achieve the set results?

1004. User: who wants the information and what are they interested in?

1005. Are the services being delivered?

1006. How well did you do?

1007. What business situation is being addressed?

1008. How is agile Data Access project management done?

1009. What is the timeline?

1010. How do you monitor progress?

1011. Purpose: toward what end is the evaluation being conducted?

1012. What good practices or successful experiences

or transferable examples have been identified?

1013. Does the solution fit in with organizations technical architectural requirements?

4.1 Project Performance Report: Data Access

1014. To what degree does the informal organization make use of individual resources and meet individual needs?

1015. To what degree does the information network provide individuals with the information they require?

1016. To what degree are fresh input and perspectives systematically caught and added (for example, through information and analysis, new members, and senior sponsors)?

1017. How can Data Access project sustainability be maintained?

1018. To what degree are the skill areas critical to team performance present?

1019. To what degree do team members articulate the teams work approach?

1020. To what degree does the funding match the requirement?

1021. To what degree are the demands of the task compatible with and converge with the mission and functions of the formal organization?

1022. To what degree is there centralized control of information sharing?

1023. To what degree does the task meet individual needs?

1024. To what degree will the team adopt a concrete, clearly understood, and agreed-upon approach that will result in achievement of the teams goals?

1025. How is the data used?

1026. To what degree will team members, individually and collectively, commit time to help themselves and others learn and develop skills?

1027. What is in it for you?

1028. To what degree does the teams work approach provide opportunity for members to engage in fact-based problem solving?

1029. To what degree does the teams approach to its work allow for modification and improvement over time?

1030. To what degree does the formal organization make use of individual resources and meet individual needs?

1031. To what degree do the goals specify concrete team work products?

4.2 Variance Analysis: Data Access

1032. Are procedures for variance analysis documented and consistently applied at the control account level and selected WBS and organizational levels at least monthly as a routine task?

1033. Contract line items and end items?

1034. What should management do?

1035. What is the expected future profitability of each customer?

1036. Historical experience?

1037. What business event causes fluctuations?

1038. Is the anticipated (firm and potential) business base Data Access projected in a rational, consistent manner?

1039. Can process improvements lead to unfavorable variances?

1040. What is exceptional?

1041. Did a new competitor enter the market?

1042. Wbs elements contractually specified for reporting of status to your organization (lowest level only)?

1043. What is your organizations rationale for sharing

expenses and services between business segments?

1044. Are the overhead pools formally and adequately identified?

1045. Are estimates of costs at completion generated in a rational, consistent manner?

1046. Are there quarterly budgets with quarterly performance comparisons?

1047. What causes selling price variance?

1048. Is the market likely to continue to grow at this rate next year?

1049. Are the actual costs used for variance analysis reconcilable with data from the accounting system?

1050. Are the requirements for all items of overhead established by rational, traceable processes?

1051. The anticipated business volume?

4.3 Earned Value Status: Data Access

1052. Are you hitting your Data Access projects targets?

1053. Verification is a process of ensuring that the developed system satisfies the stakeholders agreements and specifications; Are you building the product right? What do you verify?

1054. How does this compare with other Data Access projects?

1055. Where are your problem areas?

1056. Where is evidence-based earned value in your organization reported?

1057. Earned value can be used in almost any Data Access project situation and in almost any Data Access project environment. it may be used on large Data Access projects, medium sized Data Access projects, tiny Data Access projects (in cut-down form), complex and simple Data Access projects and in any market sector. some people, of course, know all about earned value, they have used it for years - but perhaps not as effectively as they could have?

1058. Validation is a process of ensuring that the developed system will actually achieve the stakeholders desired outcomes; Are you building the right product? What do you validate?

1059. What is the unit of forecast value?

1060. When is it going to finish?

1061. If earned value management (EVM) is so good in determining the true status of a Data Access project and Data Access project its completion, why is it that hardly any one uses it in information systems related Data Access projects?

1062. How much is it going to cost by the finish?

4.4 Risk Audit: Data Access

1063. What are the costs associated with late delivery or a defective product?

1064. Where will the next scandal or adverse media involving your organization come from?

1065. What expertise do auditors need to generate effective business-level risk assessments, and to what extent do auditors currently possess the already stated attributes?

1066. What are the differences and similarities between strategic and operational risks in your organization?

1067. Extending the consideration on the halo effect, to what extent are auditors able to build skepticism in evidence review?

1068. Is the customer technically sophisticated in the product area?

1069. Do you have a consistent repeatable process that is actually used?

1070. Number of users of the product?

1071. What can you do to manage outcomes?

1072. Does the customer have a solid idea of what is required?

1073. How risk averse are you?

1074. How effective are your risk controls?

1075. Are auditors able to effectively apply more soft evidence found in the risk-assessment process with the results of more tangible audit evidence found through more substantive testing?

1076. Are all participants informed of safety issues?

1077. Is there a screening process that will ensure all participants have the fitness and skills required to safely participate?

1078. Are risk assessments documented?

1079. Can assurance be expanded beyond the traditional audit without undermining independence?

1080. What events or circumstances could affect the achievement of your objectives?

1081. Do you have position descriptions for all office bearers/staff?

4.5 Contractor Status Report: Data Access

1082. How is risk transferred?

1083. What was the overall budget or estimated cost?

1084. What was the final actual cost?

1085. Who can list a Data Access project as organization experience, your organization or a previous employee of your organization?

1086. If applicable; describe your standard schedule for new software version releases. Are new software version releases included in the standard maintenance plan?

1087. Describe how often regular updates are made to the proposed solution. Are corresponding regular updates included in the standard maintenance plan?

1088. Are there contractual transfer concerns?

1089. How long have you been using the services?

1090. What was the actual budget or estimated cost for your organizations services?

1091. What process manages the contracts?

1092. What was the budget or estimated cost for your organizations services?

1093. What are the minimum and optimal bandwidth requirements for the proposed solution?

1094. What is the average response time for answering a support call?

4.6 Formal Acceptance: Data Access

1095. What features, practices, and processes proved to be strengths or weaknesses?

1096. Did the Data Access project manager and team act in a professional and ethical manner?

1097. What lessons were learned about your Data Access project management methodology?

1098. What function(s) does it fill or meet?

1099. Does it do what client said it would?

1100. What was done right?

1101. Was the Data Access project goal achieved?

1102. What is the Acceptance Management Process?

1103. Who supplies data?

1104. Was the Data Access project work done on time, within budget, and according to specification?

1105. Was business value realized?

1106. Was the client satisfied with the Data Access project results?

1107. Have all comments been addressed?

1108. Is formal acceptance of the Data Access project

product documented and distributed?

1109. How well did the team follow the methodology?

1110. Do you buy-in installation services?

1111. Was the Data Access project managed well?

1112. Do you perform formal acceptance or burn-in tests?

1113. General estimate of the costs and times to complete the Data Access project?

1114. Was the sponsor/customer satisfied?

5.0 Closing Process Group: Data Access

1115. What areas does the group agree are the biggest success on the Data Access project?

1116. Will the Data Access project deliverable(s) replace a current asset or group of assets?

1117. What areas were overlooked on this Data Access project?

1118. Are there funding or time constraints?

1119. What could have been improved?

1120. What were the desired outcomes?

1121. How well did the team follow the chosen processes?

1122. How well defined and documented were the Data Access project management processes you chose to use?

1123. What is the overall risk of the Data Access project to your organization?

1124. Is this an updated Data Access project Proposal Document?

1125. When will the Data Access project be done?

1126. Just how important is your work to the overall success of the Data Access project?

1127. Measurable - are the targets measurable?

1128. Can the lesson learned be replicated?

1129. Is this a follow-on to a previous Data Access project?

1130. What level of risk does the proposed budget represent to the Data Access project?

5.1 Procurement Audit: Data Access

1131. Were the documents received scrutinised for completion and adherence to stated conditions before the tenders were evaluated?

1132. Are decisions to outsource and being part of public private partnerships closely linked to the delivery of departments core services and functions?

1133. Is the foreseen budget compared with similar Data Access projects or procurements yet realised (historical standards)?

1134. Are unusual uses of organization funds investigated?

1135. Are known obligations, such as salaries and contracts, encumbered at the beginning of the year?

1136. Are travel expenditures monitored to determine that they are in line with other employees and reasonable for the area of travel?

1137. Were additional works brought about by a cause which had not previously existed?

1138. Is the chosen supplier part of your organizations database?

1139. Has the award included no items different from the already stated contained in bid specifications?

1140. Are all purchase orders signed by the

purchasing agent?

1141. When competitive dialogue was used, did the contracting authority provide sufficient justification for the use of this procedure and was the contract actually particularly complex?

1142. Are information technology resources (e-procurement) used to reduce costs?

1143. Are checks used in numeric sequence?

1144. Does procurement staff have recognized professional procurement qualifications or sufficient training?

1145. Are the internal control systems operational?

1146. Is there a record maintained of the procedures followed in the opening of tenders together with the reasons for the acceptance or rejection of tenders received?

1147. Are the right skills, experiences and competencies present in the acquisition workgroup and are the necessary outside specialists involved in part of the process?

1148. Are approvals needed if changes are made in the quantity or specification of the original purchase requisition?

1149. Was the award decision based on the result of the evaluation of tenders?

1150. Did your organization decide for an appropriate

and admissible procurement procedure?

5.2 Contract Close-Out: Data Access

1151. Parties: who is involved?

1152. Change in knowledge?

1153. Have all contract records been included in the Data Access project archives?

1154. What is capture management?

1155. How/when used ?

1156. Change in attitude or behavior?

1157. Was the contract complete without requiring numerous changes and revisions?

1158. Are the signers the authorized officials?

1159. What happens to the recipient of services?

1160. Was the contract sufficiently clear so as not to result in numerous disputes and misunderstandings?

1161. Was the contract type appropriate?

1162. Have all acceptance criteria been met prior to final payment to contractors?

1163. Parties: Authorized?

1164. Has each contract been audited to verify acceptance and delivery?

1165. Have all contracts been closed?

1166. How does it work?

1167. How is the contracting office notified of the automatic contract close-out?

1168. Have all contracts been completed?

1169. Why Outsource?

1170. Change in circumstances?

5.3 Project or Phase Close-Out: Data Access

1171. Planned completion date?

1172. What hierarchical authority does the stakeholder have in your organization?

1173. Is the lesson based on actual Data Access project experience rather than on independent research?

1174. Was the schedule met?

1175. Complete yes or no?

1176. Did the Data Access project management methodology work?

1177. What information is each stakeholder group interested in?

1178. Who is responsible for award close-out?

1179. Planned remaining costs?

1180. When and how were information needs best met?

1181. Were risks identified and mitigated?

1182. Have business partners been involved extensively, and what data was required for them?

1183. In addition to assessing whether the Data Access project was successful, it is equally critical to analyze why it was or was not fully successful. Are you including this?

1184. What were the actual outcomes?

1185. Does the lesson describe a function that would be done differently the next time?

1186. What was expected from each stakeholder?

1187. Is the lesson significant, valid, and applicable?

1188. What are the marketing communication needs for each stakeholder?

5.4 Lessons Learned: Data Access

1189. What is the impact of tax policy on the case?

1190. What did you put in place to ensure success?

1191. What other questions should you have asked?

1192. How clearly defined were the objectives for this Data Access project?

1193. What would you change?

1194. Would you spend your own time fixing this issue?

1195. What is your working hypothesis, if you have one?

1196. How many interest groups are stakeholders?

1197. What if anything has been lacking?

1198. Who needs to learn lessons?

1199. What could be done to improve the process?

1200. How useful was the content of the training you received in preparation for the use of the product/ service?

1201. What are the conceptual limits of the research?

1202. Are new goals needed?

1203. How well did the Data Access project Manager respond to questions or comments related to the Data Access project?

1204. How well were expectations met regarding the frequency and content of information that was conveyed to by the Data Access project Manager?

1205. How well do you feel the executives supported this Data Access project?

Index

staffing 25, 90, 143, 149
stages 130
standard   7, 96, 99, 121, 159, 201, 241
standards   1, 11-12, 88-89, 91, 93, 95-96, 143, 178, 180, 216, 247
started 9, 156
starting 12
stated 107, 113, 177, 186, 239, 247
statement   3, 12, 85, 140-142, 176, 209
statements   13, 26, 31, 36, 40, 56, 72, 87, 99, 119, 182
statistics   141
status 5-6, 61, 149, 170, 187-188, 194, 202, 205, 211, 221, 235, 237-238, 241
steering   132, 169, 202, 205
stopper   136
storage   182
stored 60-61, 63, 71, 134
stories 32
strategic   51, 91, 149, 239
strategies   78, 96, 114-115, 143, 169, 207, 217-218
strategy   18, 35, 51, 66, 70, 82, 85, 92, 111, 113, 150, 189, 192-193, 203, 208, 217
stratify 179
Stream 65, 68
strengths   60, 142, 203, 243
stretch 117
strict   71
strive   117
Strongly   12, 17, 27, 42, 57, 73, 88, 100, 214
structure   3, 55, 67, 75, 77, 123, 140, 144, 161, 207
Structured   71, 112
stubborn   114
stupid 117
subdivide   147
subdivided   184
subject 9-10, 37, 65, 135
Subjective   180
submit 11
submitted   11, 215
subset 17
succeed   46, 226
success   19, 26, 31-32, 34, 50, 55, 66, 81, 86, 104, 106, 109, 112, 116, 149, 209, 211, 218, 231, 245-246, 254